Fasting Unleashed

How Prayer and Fasting Destroy Strongholds and Release Breakthrough!

Expanded Second Edition

Includes A Workbook, Journal and 21-Day Guided Fast Companion

ANTHONY V JOHNSON

ACKNOWLEDGMENTS

First and foremost, to my Lord and Savior Jesus Christ—my constant guide, my refuge, and my strength. Your faithfulness has carried me through every trial, and Your Word promises, "I will never leave you nor forsake you" (Hebrews 13:5). Because of Your grace, I press forward with hope, joy, and unwavering anticipation of the day You will say, "Well done, my good and faithful servant" (Matthew 25:21).

To my beloved wife, Deborah, whose love, encouragement, and quiet strength inspire me daily. Your faith, patience, and selflessness reflect the heart of a true Woman of God, and I am forever blessed to walk this journey with you.

To my father, my hero, whose courage and dedication shaped the man I am today. I remember the early mornings at the sound of the doorbell, marking his return from yet another deployment. Resting now at Arlington National Cemetery, his legacy of honor and service continues to guide and inspire me.

To my mother, whose gentle and steadfast love remains a guiding light, even in her absence. Her memory fuels my commitment to live a life of purpose and integrity.

To Pastor Mirek and Linda Hufton of World Harvest Church (Roswell, Georgia), for their tireless leadership and devotion to guiding thousands into a closer walk with Christ. They continue to send 62 or more mission teams worldwide each year saving souls by the thousands.

To Pastor Willie Russell and Flossie, whose hands-on ministry in South Africa reminds us that faith without action is incomplete.

To Apostle Fritz Musser of Tabernacle International Church (Lawrenceville, Georgia), for equipping the saints and fostering sound teaching and leadership.

Finally, to all who have walked alongside me—family, friends, mentors, and fellow laborers in the faith—your encouragement, prayers, and example have shaped this journey. May God's blessings return to you a hundredfold.

Table of Contents

PREFACE

HOW TO USE THIS BOOK

Fasting is sacred ground. The purpose of biblical fasting is not to diet. It's not to be a religious ritual. And it is not a way to manipulate God.

Biblical fasting is a deliberate act of humbling oneself before the Lord in order to draw nearer to Him, align your heart with His will, and crucify the impulses of the flesh that war against the Spirit (Galatians 5:17).

This book is not written to impress you with spiritual stories or dramatic language. It is written to guide you carefully, biblically, and responsibly through one of the most powerful disciplines in the Christian life.

But before you begin, let me clarify how this book is meant to be used.

This Is a Guide, Not a Rulebook

Fasting in Scripture varies in length, intensity, and purpose. Jesus fasted forty days and forty nights (Matt. 4:1-11). Moses fasted forty days and forty nights (Exodus 34:28). Esther called for a three-day fast (Esther 4:16). The King of Nineveh called a total fast of not only all the people but even the livestock.

The Scripture says in Jonah 3:7-10, "And he caused it to be proclaimed and published through Nineveh by the decree of the king and his nobles, saying, Let neither man nor beast, herd nor flock, taste any thing: let them not feed, nor drink water: But let man and beast be covered with sackcloth, and cry mightily unto God: yea, let them turn every one from his evil way, and from the violence that is in their hands. Who can tell if God will turn and repent, and turn away from his fierce anger, that we perish not? And God saw their works, that they turned from their evil way; and God repented of the evil, that he had said that he would do unto them; and he did it not."

And the early church fasted before commissioning leaders (Acts 13:2–3). There is no single formula.

The purpose of this book is to help you understand biblical fasting clearly and prepare wisely. This book will help you walk through the fast responsibly and guard your heart during and after the fast. Use this book as a guide—not as a rigid law.

Begin with Your Purpose

Before you choose the length of a fast, ask yourself:

- Why am I fasting?

- What am I seeking from God?

- Is this about humility or about display?

- Is this about obedience or about proving something?

Isaiah 58 reminds us that the fast God chooses is one that loosens the bonds of wickedness and aligns us with His heart. The Scripture says in Isaiah 58:6-8, "Is not this the fast that I have chosen? to loose the bands of wickedness, to undo the heavy burdens, and to let the oppressed go free, and that ye break every yoke? Is it not to deal thy bread to the hungry, and that thou bring the poor that are cast out to thy house? when thou seest the naked, that thou cover him; and that thou hide not thyself from thine own flesh? Then shall thy light break forth as the morning, and thine health shall spring forth speedily: and thy righteousness shall go before thee; the glory of the LORD shall be thy rereward."

If your motive is self-exaltation, comparison, or spiritual pride, pause. Correct your heart before you begin. Fasting must begin with humility.

Start Where You Are

Not everyone is called to a forty-day fast. Not everyone should attempt extended fasting without wisdom and preparation. If you are new to fasting, begin with a 24-hour fast or skip one meal and dedicate that time to prayer. Of course, if you routinely skip a meal daily due to your time constraints or hectic schedule, then skip two meals. Build spiritual discipline gradually. Spiritual maturity grows through obedience, not extremism.

Read the Foundations First

Before attempting a fast, read:

- Part One (The Foundation), and

- Part Two (Preparing for a Fast)

Do not skip preparation. Many people fail in fasting not because they lack sincerity, but because they lack structure. Preparation protects you.

Use the Practical Sections During Your Fast

While you are fasting, refer to:

- The "What to Expect" chapters

- The daily rhythm suggestions

- The prayer guidance sections

- The temptation response strategies

When hunger intensifies or discouragement sets in, return to Scripture. Remember Jesus' response in Matthew 4:4: "Man shall not live by bread alone, but by every word that proceeds out of the mouth of God." Your fast is not sustained by willpower alone, it is sustained by the Word.

Pay Attention to Your Health

If you have medical conditions such as: diabetes, blood pressure concerns, eating disorders, chronic illness, pregnancy, or medication requirements, consult a physician before beginning. Fasting is a spiritual discipline—not a reckless act. Wisdom and faith work hand-in-hand.

Keep a Journal

One of the most helpful practices during a fast is journaling. Document what you are believing for, what Scripture is speaking to you, what you are experiencing emotionally, and what the Lord impresses upon your heart. Clarity often comes quietly.

Remember: Fasting Is Preparation

Fasting is not the finish line, it's a posture of consecration. Throughout the Scripture, fasting often precedes divine assignment (you will hear about my personal experience later in the book), deeper obedience, or a spiritual breakthrough. It clears the noise so you can hear clearly from the Lord. It brings about humility and sharpens sensitivity. But remember, the goal is deeper intimacy with God and faithful obedience to His leading.

Move Slowly and Reverently

Approach fasting reverently and don't boast to others. The Scripture says, "Moreover when ye fast, be not, as the hypocrites, of a sad countenance: for they disfigure their faces, that they may appear unto men to fast. Verily I say unto you, They have their reward. But thou, when thou fastest, anoint thine head, and wash thy face; That thou appear not unto men to fast, but unto thy Father which is in secret: and thy Father, which seeth in secret, shall reward thee openly" (Matt: 6:16-18). Let this discipline be between you and God. If you are ready, begin by examining your heart.

INTRODUCTION

THE BATTLE WITHIN

From the moment Adam fell in the garden of Eden, all humanity inherited a fallen nature. Every person born of the seed of man enters this world with a bent toward sin. We possess a body, a soul, and a spirit — and within us exists a conflict that Scripture describes with remarkable clarity.

The Apostle Paul writes:

> "For the flesh lusts against the Spirit, and the Spirit against the flesh: and these are contrary the one to the other: so that ye cannot do the things that ye would." (Galatians 5:17)

There is a war within every believer. The flesh craves satisfaction of its lusts, appetite, comfort, pride, indulgence, and self-will. The cravings of the flesh are often relentless. The spirit, when renewed by God, seeks to obey God, honor Him, and walk in righteousness.

Paul further explains this internal struggle in Romans 7:

> "For the good that I would I do not: but the evil which I would not, that I do... it is no more I that do it, but sin that dwelleth in me." (Romans 7:19–20)

This is not an abstract theological idea. It is daily experience. We know what is right. We want to obey. But the flesh, if not checked, resists what is right and craves pleasure and fulfillment.

How many times can you recall in your life when you knew that you should not engage in certain activity but you chose to do it anyway? How many times have you entangled yourself with an individual, perhaps a romantic interest when you knew deep down inside that you shouldn't. In many cases, friends or family warned you. But you did it anyway. And that entanglement resulted in disaster. You were being led by the flesh. The spirit warned you, but you didn't heed. It is very difficult to walk in obedience to God if you are led by the flesh. The Scripture says in 1 John 2:16,

"For all that is in the world, the lust of the flesh, and the lust of the eyes, and the pride of life, is not of the Father, but is of the world." And Galatians 5:17 says, "For the flesh lusteth against the Spirit, and the Spirit against the flesh: and these are contrary the one to the other: so that ye cannot do the things that ye would."

This tension forms the backdrop for understanding fasting.

The Origin of the Struggle

Adam was created sinless. God formed Adam from the dust of the earth and breathed into his nostrils the breath of life, and Adam became a living soul (Genesis 2:7). God then removed a rib from Adam and created the first woman, Eve. God gave a specific command that Adam should not eat *nor touch* the fruit from the tree in the midst of the garden – the tree of the knowledge of good and evil (Genesis 2:17).

Satan in the form of a serpent approached Eve while she was in the garden of Eden. The serpent struck up a conversation with Eve by initially causing her to question God's word. God previously told Adam that if he ate or touched the fruit from the tree in the midst of the garden he would surely die (Genesis 2:17).

Eve then began rationalizing and she was drawn by the appearance of the fruit. The Scripture says it was appealing to Eve's eyes.

The Scripture says in Genesis 3:6, "And when the woman saw that the tree was good for food, and that it was pleasant to the eyes, and a tree to be desired to make one wise, she took of the fruit thereof, and did eat, and gave also unto her husband with her; and he did eat."

At that very moment, sin entered the world. The "lust of the flesh, the lust of the eyes, and the pride of life" (1 John 2:16) would now characterize the human condition apart from divine grace.

Even after salvation, the believer must contend with this internal struggle. Though the spirit is made alive in Christ, the flesh remains present and must be disciplined.

God's Provision in the Battle

If the flesh relentlessly wars against the Spirit, how does the believer strengthen the Spirit? God, in His wisdom, has provided spiritual disciplines that train the soul and crucify the impulses of the flesh. Among these disciplines is fasting.

Fasting is not merely abstaining from food. It is a deliberate act of self-denial that exposes the appetites of the flesh and places the believer in a posture of humility before God.

When we fast:

- We confront our dependency on physical comfort.

- We quiet external noise.

- We acknowledge that God is our sustainer.

- We humble ourselves under His authority.

Fasting is not a form of punishment, it is alignment. It is not starvation, it is consecration. It is not self-harm, it is self-discipline.

The Purpose of This Book

This book is not written to promote extremism, sensationalism, or spiritual pride. It is written to clarify what Scripture teaches about fasting and provide practical and responsible guidance. This book is written to help believers prepare wisely, encourage spiritual maturity, guard against imbalance and deception, and show how fasting strengthens intimacy with God.

Fasting is powerful — but only when it is rooted in Scripture, guided by humility, and practiced with wisdom.

As we explore the biblical principles of fasting in the chapters that follow, we will uncover not only its profound purpose, but also its proper practice. The goal is not merely to abstain from food. The goal is to draw near to God.

PART I

THE FOUNDATION OF THE FAST

CHAPTER ONE

PURPOSE OF THE FAST

Now that we have an understanding of how sin entered the earth, and we further understand that we are born with a sin nature, let's explore the purpose of the fast. The struggle between flesh and Spirit has been established. The question now becomes: What does fasting actually accomplish?

Fasting Reorders Our Appetites

First, you should take note that Jesus did not perform any miracles prior to his baptism which was immediately followed by forty days and nights of fasting in the wilderness. Jesus did not have a sin nature. He was sinless, and He was God in the flesh. Yet it was necessary for Him to fast. The Scripture says that immediately after being baptized by John the Baptist the Holy Spirit drove Jesus into the wilderness where Jesus fasted for forty days and nights and was tempted by the devil (Matthew 4:2-4). We are, on the other hand, born with a sinful nature. How much more is the importance that we fast?

Another point to remember is that the temptation that Jesus encountered did not begin until after forty days and forty nights of fasting when Jesus was physically weak. Satan appeared to Jesus and attempted to manipulate and misquote the Word (as he did with Eve). The devil ultimately attempted to tempt Jesus with all of the wealth and glory of the world (Matthew 4:2-4). This is evident that Satan indeed had the power and authority to offer wealth and success as the "god of this world". In my book "PSYOPS: The Spiritual Battle for Your Mind and Your Soul!" I go into further detail on the devil and his tactics, including Satan's ability to bless people with wealth and success in exchange for their souls.

Fasting Exposes What Controls You

Many believers do not realize what controls them until they attempt to fast. Suddenly irritability increases, impatience rises, distractions multiply, and temptations intensify. Fasting does not create these things, it reveals them. Your body craves food, so when you begin a fast you are often immediately confronted with the aroma of food being prepared or the smell of food while you are out in public. Your flesh cries out to be fed, and you may find your mind quickly suggesting, "I should wait until tomorrow to start my fast." And your mind begins to rationalize. What you cannot say "no" to owns you. Isaiah 58 makes this clear:

> "Is not this the fast that I have chosen… to loose the bands of wickedness… to undo heavy burdens… to let the oppressed go free…"

The fast loosens spiritual bonds not because hunger earns power — but because humility invites grace.

Fasting Produces Humility

Throughout Scripture, fasting is consistently associated with humility. Nineveh fasted in repentance. In Jonah 3:6-9, the Scripture says, "For word came unto the king of Nineveh, and he arose from his throne, and he laid his robe from him, and covered him with sackcloth, and sat in ashes. And he caused it to be proclaimed and published through Nineveh by the decree of the king and his nobles, saying, Let neither man nor beast, herd nor flock, taste anything: let them not feed, nor drink water: But let man and beast be covered with sackcloth, and cry mightily unto God: yea, let them turn every one from his evil way, and from the violence that is in their hands. Who can tell if God will turn and repent, and turn away from his fierce anger, that we perish not?"

In this Scripture, the Prophet Jonah prophesied that Nineveh would be overthrown in forty days (Jonah 3:4). The people believed God and proclaimed a fast. Their fast was so focused that no one, not even the animals were allowed to eat anything or even drink water.

In the end, the Scripture says in Jonah 3:10, "And God saw their works, that they turned from their evil way; and God repented of the evil, that he had said that he would do unto them; and he did it not." As a result of their humility demonstrated through prayer and fasting, Nineveh was not overthrown.

Ahab fasted in fear and remorse. In 1 King 21-22, the Scripture says that Ahab heard the Word of the Lord which said, "Behold, I will bring evil upon thee, and will take away thy posterity, and will cut off from Ahab…And will make thine house like the house of Jeroboam the son of Nebat, and like the house of Baasha the son of Ahijah, for the provocation wherewith thou hast provoked me to anger, and made Israel to sin."

The Scripture says, "But there was none like unto Ahab, which did sell himself to work wickedness in the sight of the LORD, whom Jezebel his wife stirred up. And he did very abominably in following idols, according to all things as did the Amorites, whom the LORD cast out before the children of Israel" (1 King 21:25-26).

Ahab fasted. The Scripture says, "And it came to pass, when Ahab heard those words, that he rent his clothes, and put sackcloth upon his flesh, and fasted, and lay in sackcloth, and went softly. And the word of the LORD came to Elijah the Tishbite, saying, Seest thou how Ahab humbleth himself before me? because he humbleth himself before me, I will not bring the evil in his days: but in his son's days will I bring the evil upon his house" (1 Kings 27-29).

Ezra fasted for protection. In Ezra 8:21, the Scripture says, "Then I proclaimed a fast there, at the river of Ahava, that we might afflict ourselves before our God, to seek of him a right way for us, and for our little ones, and for all our substance."

Esther fasted for divine favor after Haman plotted to destroy the Jews. Esther told Mordecai, "Go, gather together all the Jews that are present in Shushan, and fast ye for me, and neither eat nor drink three days, night or day: I also and my maidens will fast likewise; and so will I go in unto the king, which is not according to the law: and if I perish, I perish" (Esther 4:16). As a result, Esther found favor with the king and the Jews were spared.

Joel called for fasting in national repentance. The Scripture says, "Therefore also now, saith the LORD, turn ye even to me with all your heart, and with fasting, and with weeping, and with mourning: And rend your heart, and not your garments, and turn unto the LORD your God: for He is gracious and merciful, slow to anger, and of great kindness, and repenteth Him of the evil" (Joel 2:12-13).

There was a further cry to, "Sanctify ye a fast, call a solemn assembly, gather the elders and all the inhabitants of the land into the house of the LORD your God, and cry unto the LORD" (Joel 1:14).

Fasting says "I am dependent." It strips away pride and silences self-sufficiency.

Psalm 35:13 says: "I humbled my soul with fasting." Not my body — my soul. Fasting humbles the inner man.

Fasting Intensifies Spiritual Clarity

The Scripture in Isaiah 58:6 proclaims that this is the fast that God has chosen to loose the bands of wickedness… It is a sobering reminder of the importance of the fast. In Mark 9, the disciples could not cast a demonic spirit out of a man. When they inquired of Jesus as to why they could not cast the demon out, Jesus said: "This kind can come forth by nothing, but by prayer and fasting" (Matthew 17:21, Mark 9:29).

There are dimensions of spiritual authority that are strengthened through disciplined communion with God. But notice, fasting should always be accompanied by prayer. Jesus did not say fasting replaces prayer. He joined them together. Prayer is communication. Fasting is consecration. When combined, they sharpen spiritual sensitivity.

Fasting Aligns You with God's Will

Moses fasted forty days before receiving the Law (Exodus 34). Jesus fasted before launching His public ministry. The early church fasted before sending out Paul and Barnabas (Acts 13:2–3).

Fasting often precedes: direction, commissioning, breakthrough, and revelation. It creates space to hear clearly not because God speaks louder — but because we listen better.

Fasting Is Not About Dieting or Detox

It must be stated clearly; biblical fasting is not:

- Weight loss
- Intermittent fasting for health
- Juice cleanses
- Detox Regimen

Those may have physical benefits, but the biblical fast is spiritual in purpose. Isaiah 58 rebukes those who fast externally but remain unchanged internally. The fast God chooses is one that transforms the heart.

The Central Purpose

To summarize, fasting exists to:

- Subdue the flesh
- Humble the soul
- Sharpen spiritual sensitivity
- Break spiritual bondage
- Seek divine direction
- Draw near to God

The goal is not power, experience, or the supernatural. It is intimacy, obedience and surrender.

CHAPTER REVIEW

This chapter introduces the purpose of biblical fasting within the larger struggle between the flesh and the Spirit. Because humanity is born with a sin nature, believers experience an ongoing tension between spiritual obedience and physical appetite. Fasting addresses this conflict directly. By temporarily denying the desires of the body, the believer intentionally reorders priorities and learns dependence upon God. The fast does not change God's will; rather, it disciplines the believer and strengthens spiritual attentiveness.

KEY SCRIPTURES

- Galatians 5:16–17
- Matthew 4:4
- Romans 7:18–25
- Joel 2:12
- Isaiah 58:6

DISCUSSION QUESTIONS

(For Groups)

1. How does fasting address the conflict between the flesh and the Spirit described in Scripture?
2. Why do you think God designed spiritual disciplines that involve physical sacrifice?
3. In what ways can fasting help believers recognize the influence of the flesh in their lives?
4. How does understanding the purpose of fasting prevent it from becoming merely religious routine?

PERSONAL REFLECTION

1. Where do you most experience the tension between spiritual desire and physical appetite?

____

____

____

____

2. How might fasting help you recognize areas where the flesh has greater influence than it should?_

----

3. What would it look like for your life to be more governed by the Spirit than by natural impulses?

JOURNAL BEFORE THE LORD

Write your prayer, reflections, and commitments below.

CHAPTER TWO

PROPER METHODS OF FASTING

Now, in addressing the proper methods of fasting, it should be emphasized that we are dealing with scripturally based, biblical fasting. As seen in several Scriptures, every Scripture points out that biblical fasting involves the **complete and total abstinence from food**. Several Scriptures even highlight abstaining from both food and water. So, there is no biblical fast mentioned in the Scripture in which the people consumed any form of food during the fast.

And this brings us to the myth of the "Daniel Fast". If you carefully review the Scripture in Daniel, it will be abundantly clear that Daniel was never fasting while abstaining from eating the king's meat or drinking the king's wine.

The Scripture states, "But Daniel purposed in his heart that he would not defile himself with the portion of the king's meat, nor with the wine which he drank: therefore, he requested of the prince of the eunuchs that he might not defile himself" (Daniel 1:8).

"Now God had brought Daniel into favor and tender love with the prince of the eunuchs. And the prince of the eunuchs said unto Daniel, I fear my lord the king, who hath appointed your meat and your drink: for why should he see your faces worse liking than the children which are of your sort? Then shall ye make me endanger my head to the king. Then said Daniel to Melzar, whom the prince of the eunuchs had set over Daniel, Hananiah, Mishael, and Azariah, prove thy servants, I beseech thee, ten days; and let them give us pulse to eat, and water to drink. Then let our countenances be looked upon before thee, and the countenance of the children that eat of the portion of the king's meat: and as thou seest, deal with thy servants.

So he consented to them in this matter, and proved them ten days. And at the end of ten days their countenances appeared fairer and fatter in flesh than all the children which did eat the portion of the king's meat. Thus, Melzar took away the portion of their meat, and the wine that they should drink; and gave them pulse" (Daniel 1:8-16).

I recall when I was eight years old, I was sitting at the kitchen table. My mother had prepared pig's feet for dinner. And when I attempted to wipe my hands with a napkin, the napkin tore and was stuck to my hands. I said at that very moment, "I am never going to eat pig's feet again!" And I never ate or touched pig's feet since that day. Does that mean I was "fasting" from eating pig's feet? NO! It simply means that I don't eat pig's feet.

Likewise, Daniel was not fasting at all. Again, let's stick to the Scripture and not traditions and doctrines of men. The Scripture clearly states that Daniel purposed in his heart that he would not defile himself with the king's meat, nor with the wine the king drank. At no time in the Scripture did Daniel EVER eat of the king's meat. So, Daniel was not fasting. For religious and dietary purposes, Daniel simply refused to eat the king's meat and drink the king's wine.

Therefore, "Melzar took away the portion of their meat, and the wine that they should drink; and gave them pulse" (Daniel 1:16). Daniel ate pulse (vegetables and fruit) for ten days. Melzar saw that Daniel's countenance was better than those who ate the king's meat. So Melzar no longer attempted to serve Daniel the king's meat and wine. Instead, Melzar continued to serve Daniel pulse (vegetables and fruit).

Fasting means to completely abstain from eating food. The fast is broken when a person returns to eating food again. And, as seen throughout the Scripture, every fast lasted a set number of days and sometimes nights.

When you fast, you are crucifying your flesh. There are many people who engage in fruit and vegetable diets for health purposes such as weight loss or detoxing, etc. However, eating fruits and vegetables does not fit the definition of a biblical fast.

Now, before starting a fast, it is recommended that you consult a physician if you have any health-related issues of concern. There is no set rule as to how long you should fast. Esther fasted for three days. Jesus and Moses fasted for forty days and nights. The king of Nineveh called for a three day fast. You should seek the Lord for direction. So, let's explore some practical tips for fasting:

Understand your Purpose for Fasting

Remember, biblical fasting is NOT about losing weight or detoxing. Instead, your purpose for fasting should be:

- Drawing closer to God.
- Humbling yourself before God (Psalm 35:13).
- Seeking a spiritual breakthrough (Isaiah 58:6).
- Aligning your spirit with God's will; and
- Repenting and interceding for others.

Throughout your fast, meditate on key Scriptures about fasting, such as Isaiah 58, Matthew 6:16-18, and Joel 2:12-13, so that your fast will be grounded in the Word of God.

Prepare Yourself Spiritually

Before you begin your fast, pray. Ask God for strength, wisdom, and clarity about the goals of your fast. Confess your sins and repent. Ask God to cleanse your heart. (1 John 1:9). And, determine the type and duration of your fast in prayer while seeking God's guidance.

Determine the Type of Fast

Is your fast going to be a COMPLETE FAST in which you will abstain from ALL food and drink (e.g., water) for a specified period? (Esther 4:16, Jonah 3:7). Is your fast going to be a PARTIAL/INTERMITTENT FAST in which you are abstaining from certain meals (i.e., skipping meals during certain times of the day to dedicate your time to prayer and meditation); or

A WATER-ONLY FAST in which you are drinking water while avoiding all food (Matthew 4:2).

Set a Specific Time Frame

Start small, especially if you are new to fasting (e.g., skip one meal or fast for a full day).

Build up to longer fasts (3, 7, 21, or 40 days) as you grow spiritually. And avoid unrealistic commitments that may discourage you.

Prioritize Prayer with the Word of God

Make time for prayer. Schedule daily prayer where you spend time with God during your usual meal times. And engage in Scripture study. Focus on versus about dependence on God, repentance, and breakthrough. And spend time in worship and meditation. Sing songs of praise and reflect on God's promises. Listen to "anointed" worship music, not entertainment.

Stay Physically Prepared

Hydrate if your fast allows water. Drink plenty of water to stay healthy. And ease into your fast. Eat lighter meals before starting your fast. Don't overeat. Know your limits, and consult a physician if you have medical issues.

And then gradually break the fast. Reintroduce food slowly to avoid shocking your system.

Avoid Distractions

Reduce or eliminate entertainment, social media or other distractions. Create a peaceful environment for prayer and reflection. And remember, fast in secret. Don't seek validation from others (Matthew 6:16-18).

Persevere Through Challenges

Anticipate spiritual resistance or increased temptation as your flesh reacts to being denied food (Galatians 5:17). Combat hunger or discouragement with Scripture (Matthew 4:4: "Man shall not live by bread alone..."). And ask the Holy Spirit for strength when feeling weak.

Trust God for the Results

Spiritual breakthroughs might not come immediately. Trust that God is working and be patient (Isaiah 40:31). Seek God's will above your personal desires and remain humble. Document your thoughts, prayers, and answered prayers in a journal during your fast. This can help you see how God is moving on your behalf.

End Your Fast with Gratitude and Reflection

Thank God for sustaining you throughout the fast. Reflect on your spiritual journey; what you learned spiritually and emotionally; and maintain any new spiritual disciplines such as: praying more frequently or engaging in a deeper study of the Scripture in your daily life. Fasting, when done with the right heart and purpose can bring transformation, deliverance, and renewed intimacy with God. Keep your focus on God, and He will honor your obedience and sacrifice!

CHAPTER REVIEW

This chapter examines the biblical method of fasting and emphasizes that Scripture consistently describes fasting as abstaining from food. While modern culture has introduced many variations, the biblical pattern remains clear. Fasting is not primarily about comfort or convenience; it involves genuine physical sacrifice. Understanding the scriptural model protects believers from redefining fasting according to preference rather than biblical precedent.

KEY SCRIPTURES

- Matthew 4:2
- Esther 4:16
- Acts 13:2–3
- Jonah 3:7–10
- Daniel 9:3

DISCUSSION QUESTIONS

(For Groups)

1. Why is it important to define fasting according to Scripture rather than cultural trends?
2. What challenges might believers face when attempting a biblical fast?
3. How can churches teach fasting responsibly while avoiding extremes?
4. How does physical sacrifice affect spiritual focus?

PERSONAL REFLECTION

1. What concerns or obstacles come to mind when you consider a biblical fast?

____

____

____

____

2. How might preparing spiritually and physically help you approach fasting wisely?

____

____

____

____

3. What adjustments would help you pursue fasting with sincerity rather than pressure or obligation?

____

____

____

____

JOURNAL BEFORE THE LORD

Write your prayer, reflections, and commitments below.

PART II

THE INNER WORK OF FASTING

CHAPTER THREE

Spirit, Soul, and Body: What Happens When You Fast?

Fasting is not merely an outward act. It is an inward reordering. To understand what truly happens when a believer fasts, we must first understand the nature of man as revealed in Scripture.

Paul writes:

"And the very God of peace sanctify you wholly; and I pray God your whole spirit and soul and body be preserved blameless…" (1 Thessalonians 5:23).

Scripture reveals that man is tripartite — spirit, soul, and body. The body connects us to the physical world. The soul encompasses mind, will, and emotions. And the spirit is the part of man that communes with God. Fasting impacts all three.

The Body: Confronting Appetite

The body itself is not evil. It is created by God. But it is fallen as a result of Adam's sin. Our bodies demand food and sleep. Our flesh demands comfort, pleasure and relief. And when these desires remain unchecked, they dominate the soul.

The Apostle Paul said:

"I keep under my body, and bring it into subjection…" (1 Corinthians 9:27).

Fasting is one of the most direct ways to bring the body into subjection. When you refuse food, your body protests. Hunger becomes loud. You may experience headaches, and your energy fluctuates. In those moments, a confrontation occurs. Will the body rule or will the spirit rule? Fasting trains the body to obey. It reminds the flesh that it is not the master.

The Soul: Exposure and Purification

Many believers are surprised by what surfaces during a fast: irritation, restlessness, emotional volatility, anxiety, distraction. Have you ever noticed how some people become cranky if they miss one meal?

Food is often used as comfort, a distraction, for emotional regulation or reward. And when it is removed, the soul is exposed. Fasting acts like a mirror. It reveals what you run to, what you depend on, and what controls your emotional state.

Psalm 35:13 says: "I humbled my soul with fasting."

It is not just the body that's affected, it's the soul. Humbling the soul means surrendering the will. It means allowing God to confront pride, resentment, fear, and self-reliance.

During fasting, the mind often becomes clearer — not because of mysticism, but because noise is reduced. Meals take time. Preparation takes energy. And consumption requires attention.

When that cycle pauses, space is created. Space allows reflection. Reflection allows repentance. And repentance allows renewal.

The Spirit: Heightened Sensitivity

The spirit of man, when born again, is alive unto God. However, spiritual sensitivity can be dulled by:

- Constant distraction
- Entertainment saturation
- Excessive indulgence
- Busyness
- Emotional overload

Fasting does not make God speak louder. It makes the believer quieter.

Jesus said:

"Man shall not live by bread alone, but by every word that proceedeth out of the mouth of God" (Matthew 4:4).

When physical sustenance is temporarily suspended, spiritual hunger intensifies. Scripture becomes sharper. Conviction becomes clearer. And prayer becomes more focused.

This is not automatic. It requires intention. But fasting creates the conditions for spiritual attentiveness.

Alignment, Not Manipulation

It must be stated clearly: Fasting does not force God to act. It does not earn favor in and of itself, although there are several instances mentioned in the Scripture in which because of their humility while fasting, God spared certain people or even nations from punishment.

Fasting does not twist Heaven's arm. Instead, it aligns the believer with God's will.

When Ezra proclaimed a fast (Ezra 8:21), it was:

"that we might afflict ourselves before our God, to seek of him a right way…"

The fast is not to control circumstances. It is used to seek direction. The believer who fasts with the intention of manipulating outcomes misunderstands the purpose. Fasting is surrender.

What Fasting Does Over Time

Short fasts teach discipline. Extended fasts reveal deeper layers of dependency. And over time, fasting produces: increased self-control, heightened discernment, greater patience, deeper humility, and a stronger prayer life.

Fasting builds spiritual stamina. Resolve is strengthened, and it cultivates restraint. These qualities are not dramatic — but they are powerful.

A Warning About Imbalance

As the body weakens, emotions can intensify. Thoughts may feel more vivid. Spiritual impressions may seem stronger. However, not every impression is divine. This is why fasting must remain anchored in Scripture.

The spirit is strengthened — but the mind must remain sober. Physical weakness is not proof of spiritual power. Spiritual maturity is proven by fruit: love, joy, peace, patience, and self-control (Galatians 5:22–23).

If fasting produces pride, irritability, or superiority, something is misaligned. True fasting produces humility.

The Inner Exchange

When it comes to fasting, you exchange:

- Comfort for clarity.

- Appetite for attentiveness.

- Noise for stillness.

- Independence for dependence.

The body decreases. The spirit becomes more attentive. The soul is confronted. And God works quietly in the hidden places.

Transition

If fasting affects spirit, soul, and body so deeply, it is no surprise that throughout Scripture it often preceded moments of national and personal breakthrough.

In the next chapter, we will examine biblical accounts where fasting changed the course of history.

CHAPTER REVIEW

This chapter explains how fasting affects the entire person—spirit, soul, and body. Scripture teaches that human beings are not merely physical but are composed of multiple dimensions that influence one another. When the body is disciplined through fasting, the soul becomes more transparent and the spirit becomes more attentive to God. Understanding this relationship helps believers recognize why fasting often brings deeper spiritual awareness.

KEY SCRIPTURES

- 1 Thessalonians 5:23
- Hebrews 4:12
- Galatians 5:16
- Psalm 42:1–2
- Romans 12:1

DISCUSSION QUESTIONS

(For Groups)

1. How does Scripture describe the relationship between the spirit, soul, and body?
2. Why might fasting increase a believer's awareness of spiritual realities?
3. What role does self-control play in spiritual maturity?
4. How can believers maintain balance while pursuing spiritual sensitivity?

PERSONAL REFLECTION

1. In which area—spirit, soul, or body—do you feel most out of alignment with God?

____

____

____

____

2. How might fasting reveal hidden attitudes or habits within your soul?

____

____

____

____

3. What practices help you maintain spiritual balance while pursuing deeper devotion?

____

____

____

____

JOURNAL BEFORE THE LORD

Write your prayer, reflections, and commitments below.

CHAPTER FOUR

When Fasting Changed History

Fasting is not a minor theme in Scripture. It is not an obscure practice mentioned only once or twice. It appears repeatedly at critical moments — moments when destinies shifted, nations were preserved, revelation was given, and missions were launched.

When we examine the biblical record carefully, we discover a pattern: Fasting often precedes decisive divine intervention. But it never replaces obedience. And it does not substitute for righteousness. Fasting frequently accompanies seasons of turning, breakthrough, and direction.

Let us examine several pivotal moments in Scripture where fasting altered outcomes.

Moses: Fasting Before Revelation

In Exodus 34:28, we read:

"And he was there with the LORD forty days and forty nights; he did neither eat bread, nor drink water. And he wrote upon the tables the words of the covenant..."

Moses did not fast casually. He fasted in the presence of God while receiving covenantal revelation. This was not a crisis fast. It was a consecration fast. Forty days without food or water is not humanly sustainable without divine sustenance. This was supernatural preservation for a supernatural assignment.

Notice the sequence:

- Moses ascends to the top of the mountain.

- Moses fasts.

- God speaks.

- Covenant law is given.

Revelation followed consecration.

Moses' fast was not about repentance or deliverance. It was about alignment before receiving instruction. When God entrusts responsibility, He often prepares the vessel through separation.

Nineveh: Fasting That Averted Judgment

In Jonah 3, the prophet declared:

"Yet forty days, and Nineveh shall be overthrown."

The response was immediate. The people believed God. The king proclaimed a fast. They put on sackcloth. From the king to the lowest servant — even the animals were included in the fast. The king declared that no one, *not even the animals* would be allowed to *eat or drink* anything during the fast.

This was corporate repentance. They didn't argue theology. They didn't negotiate terms. They humbled themselves.

And Scripture records:

"And God saw their works, that they turned from their evil way; and God repented of the evil..." (Jonah 3:10).

Notice something important: The fast was accompanied by action. They turned from violence. They changed behavior. And they repented.

Fasting without repentance would have meant nothing. But fasting with humility moved the heart of God. Judgment was suspended, and history changed.

Esther: Fasting Before Risk

In Esther 4, a decree had gone forth to annihilate the Jewish people. Haman's plot was set. The law of the Medes and Persians could not easily be reversed.

Esther faced a dilemma:

Approach the king uninvited and risk death — Or remain silent and watch her people perish.

Before she acted, she called for a fast:

"Fast ye for me, and neither eat nor drink three days, night or day..."

She did not rush into confrontation. She did not rely solely on courage. She sought divine favor.

Three days later, she entered the king's court. The result: Favor. Reversal. Deliverance.

Fasting preceded strategic action. The fast did not eliminate the risk — but it prepared the heart and positioned her for grace.

Ezra: Fasting for Protection

Ezra 8:21 says:

"Then I proclaimed a fast... that we might afflict ourselves before our God, to seek of him a right way..."

Ezra was leading people through dangerous territory. Bandits, threats, vulnerability — all were real concerns. He refused to request a military escort because he had declared publicly that God's hand was upon them.

Instead, he proclaimed a fast.

The fast was for: direction, protection, and divine covering.

The result?

"So we fasted and besought our God... and he was intreated of us."

Again, fasting preceded movement. Before the journey, they humbled themselves.

Daniel: Fasting for Understanding

In Daniel 9, Daniel understood by the books that seventy years of desolation were nearly complete.

What did Daniel do? The Scripture says, in Daniel 9:3,

"I set my face unto the Lord God, to seek by prayer and supplications, with fasting..."

Daniel's fast was intercessory. He confessed national sin. He repented on behalf of the people, and he sought understanding.

In Daniel 10, another fast is recorded — this time a three-week partial fast accompanied by mourning and prayer. The Scripture says,

"In those days I Daniel was mourning three full weeks. I ate no pleasant bread, neither came flesh nor wine in my mouth, neither did I anoint myself at all, till three whole weeks were fulfilled" (Daniel 10: 2-3).

After twenty-one days, angelic visitation came. The messenger revealed that spiritual resistance had been present — a conflict in the unseen realm.

Daniel's fasting did not create the battle — but it coincided with persistent intercession until breakthrough manifested. Fasting here is linked with: perseverance, spiritual clarity and revelation.

The Early Church: Fasting Before Mission

Acts 13 records a critical turning point in church history:

"As they ministered to the Lord, and fasted, the Holy Ghost said, Separate me Barnabas and Saul..." (Acts 13:2).

The church in Antioch was not facing persecution at that moment. They were worshiping, ministering and fasting. And, in that environment of devotion, the Holy Spirit spoke. Paul and Barnabas were commissioned, and the missionary movement began. The gospel spread into the Gentile world.

Fasting here precedes sending. It is preparation before expansion.

A Pattern Emerges

When we place these examples side by side, a consistent pattern appears:

Fasting often precedes:

- Revelation (Moses)

- Repentance and mercy (Nineveh)

- Strategic breakthrough (Esther)

- Protection and direction (Ezra)
- Spiritual understanding (Daniel)
- Mission and expansion (Acts 13)

In each case, fasting was accompanied by prayer, humility, turning of the heart and action. Fasting alone accomplishes nothing without combining it with repentance, humility, and prayer. Fasting joined with repentance and obedience shifts outcomes.

What Fasting Does Not Guarantee

It must be stated carefully: not every fast produces immediate visible results. The Bible records victories — but it also records waiting. Fasting is not a formula. It is posture.

Sometimes the breakthrough is internal before it becomes external. Sometimes the answer is clarity rather than change. Sometimes God strengthens the believer rather than altering circumstances.

The purpose is not to guarantee a particular outcome — but to position oneself rightly before God.

Why These Stories Matter

These accounts are not recorded for inspiration alone. They reveal principles. They teach us that God responds to humility. Consecration prepares the heart for instruction. Fasting sharpens discernment.

Spiritual battles are often unseen. National and personal turning points often follow seasons

of affliction before God. If fasting was consistently present at moments of historical shift, we should not treat it lightly. Fasting is not outdated, and it is not ceremonial. Fasting remains a discipline that aligns the believer with divine purpose.

The Thread That Connects Them All

In every example, fasting was never about self-exaltation. It was about dependence. Moses depended on revelation. Nineveh depended on mercy. Esther depended on favor. Ezra depended on protection.

Daniel depended on understanding. The early church depended on direction.

Dependence is the common denominator, and dependence is the foundation of spiritual maturity.

Transition

If fasting has played such a significant role throughout biblical history, we must examine another critical truth: fasting was never meant to stand alone. In every case, it was joined with prayer.

In the next chapter, we will explore the inseparable partnership between prayer and fasting — and why separating the two weakens both.

CHAPTER REVIEW

This chapter demonstrates that fasting has often appeared at decisive moments in biblical history. From Moses to Esther to the early church, fasting accompanied critical events where God's people sought direction, deliverance, or divine intervention. These examples reveal that fasting was not an occasional ritual but a meaningful response when believers sought God's guidance during pivotal moments.

KEY SCRIPTURES

- Exodus 34:28
- Esther 4:16
- Jonah 3:5–10
- Acts 13:2–3
- Acts 14:23

DISCUSSION QUESTIONS

(For Groups)

1. What biblical examples of fasting stood out to you most in this chapter?
2. Why do you think fasting often appears at critical turning points in Scripture?
3. How might fasting help believers seek God during important decisions today?
4. What can modern churches learn from these historical examples?

PERSONAL REFLECTION

1. Are there situations in your life where seeking God through fasting might be appropriate?

____

____

____

____

2. How might fasting help you approach difficult decisions with greater spiritual clarity?

____

____

____

____

3. What lessons from biblical history encourage you to trust God more deeply?

____

____

____

JOURNAL BEFORE THE LORD

Write your prayer, reflections, and commitments below.

CHAPTER FIVE

Prayer and Fasting: The Divine Partnership

Throughout Scripture, fasting is rarely mentioned alone. It is almost always joined with prayer. The two are not identical — but they are inseparable. Fasting without prayer becomes dieting. Prayer without discipline often becomes distracting. When combined, they create spiritual focus. To understand fasting correctly, we must understand its partnership with prayer.

Jesus Assumed Both

In Matthew 6, Jesus did not command fasting as a novelty. He spoke of it as an expectation:

"When ye fast…"
"When ye pray…"

Notice the wording. Not if, but "when".

Jesus assumed His followers would pray. He also assumed they would fast. But He warned against hypocrisy. The Pharisees fasted publicly to appear spiritual. They disfigured their faces and sought attention.

Jesus corrected this by teaching how to behave when fasting. Jesus said, when you fast:

"Anoint thine head, and wash thy face; That thou appear not unto men to fast…"

(Matthew 6:17-18).

Fasting, like prayer, is directed toward God — not toward observers. The power lies not in the performance, but in the posture.

What Prayer Does

Prayer is communication with God. It includes:

- Worship
- Petition
- Intercession
- Thanksgiving, and
- Repentance

Through prayer, the believer:

- Expresses dependence
- Aligns desires
- Seeks guidance
- Confesses sin, and
- Asks for intervention

Prayers engage the will. It focuses the mind, and it directs the heart. But prayer alone can sometimes remain surface-level if distractions dominate.

What Fasting Adds

Fasting intensifies focus. When the body is denied food, the believer becomes more aware of weakness and dependence. Hunger is a constant reminder, and every physical craving becomes an invitation to pray.

So, instead of focusing on "I am hungry," focus on "Lord, I hunger for You." Instead of reaching for food, one reaches for Scripture. Fasting redirects appetite. It converts physical desire into spiritual attentiveness.

Mark 9: The Combined Authority

In Mark 9, a father brought his demon-possessed son to the disciples. However, the disciples could not cast the demon out. After Jesus delivered the boy, the disciples asked privately:

"Why could not we cast him out?" Jesus responded, "This kind can come forth by nothing, but by prayer and fasting."

The authority was not mechanical. It was relational. Prayer builds relationship, and fasting deepens surrender. Together, they strengthen spiritual authority.

Notice what Jesus did not say. Jesus did not say that fasting alone drives out demons. He did not say technique drives out demons. He pointed to spiritual depth Some situations require deeper alignment.

Why Fasting Without Prayer Is Empty

It must be plainly stated: abstaining from food without seeking God is pointless spiritually.

If you fast but don't pray, don't read Scripture, don't repent and don't seek God, you have simply endured hunger.

Isaiah 58 rebukes Israel for fasting outwardly while continuing injustice and strife.

God asked:

"Is not this the fast that I have chosen? to loose the bands of wickedness, to undo the heavy burdens, and to let the oppressed go free, and that ye break every yoke?" (Isaiah 58:6-7). The people were going through the motions — but their hearts remained unchanged.

Fasting must be accompanied by self-examination, repentance, communion and transformation. Otherwise, it becomes religious exercise.

Why Prayer Without Discipline Weakens Focus

Prayers are powerful. But in a culture saturated with distractions, prayer often competes with emails, text messages, notifications, responsibilities, social media, entertainment, fatigue, work schedules, and noise.

Fasting removes one major cycle of daily distraction — eating. Meals structure the day. Preparation requires time. Consumption occupies attention especially when accompanied by friendships, family or co-workers.

When that cycle pauses, space emerges. Space strengthens prayer. Fasting does not replace prayer — it creates room for it.

The Internal Exchange

When prayer and fasting operate together, something shifts internally. The lust of the flesh, lust of the eyes and pride of life decrease. Addictions and strongholds are broken. The spirit becomes attentive. The soul becomes transparent before God. Discipline replaces indulgence. And dependence replaces self-reliance. It's not dramatic outwardly — but inwardly it is powerful.

Prayer During Fasting: What It Should Include

Prayer during fasting should be intentional, and it should include a combination of:

It should include:

- Worship – acknowledging God's holiness.
- Repentance – allowing God to search the heart.
- Intercession – standing in the gap for others.
- Listening – creating silence for reflection.

- Scripture meditation – grounding impressions in truth.

Fasting without Scripture can drift into subjectivity. Scripture anchors experience, and the Word guards the mind.

Avoiding Emotional Extremes

Here's something to remember: During fasting, emotions may intensify. Physical weakness can amplify feelings. And some may mistake emotional intensity for spiritual revelation.

But, remain steady, calm and scripturally rooted during fasting. If you experience pride, irritability, feel spiritually superior, or if fasting produces isolation, then something is misaligned. The fruit of true communion is humility and love.

Corporate Prayer and Fasting

Throughout Scripture, there were seasons of corporate fasting. Nineveh was the capital city of the Neo-Assyrian Empire located on the eastern bank of the Tigris River. When Jonah delivered the word from the Lord that Nineveh would be overthrown, the King called a corporate fast. No one was permitted to each or even drink anything, including the animals. The early church fasted together. Esther called a communal fast.

Corporate fasting produces unity, shared humility, collective repentance, and spiritual clarity. But it must never become a competition. Spiritual disciplines are not measurements of worth. They are expressions of surrender.

Private Devotion and Hidden Discipline

Jesus emphasized secrecy in fasting; private prayer, consecration and discipline. There are seasons for corporate fasting — but the foundation must be private devotion. God often works most deeply in hidden places. What is done quietly shapes what is lived publicly.

The Balance Between Intensity and Sustainability

Not every season requires extended fasting. And as you can see from the periods of fasting in the Scripture, not every breakthrough requires forty days. Take Esther for example. The Jews were spared after a three-day fast. What is required when it comes to fasting is wisdom. Prayer should guide fasting — not pressure or comparison.

As a believer, ask "Why am I fasting?" Seek the Lord's leading and examine your heart. The purpose is alignment — not endurance contests.

The Ultimate Aim

Prayer and fasting together aim at one thing: intimacy with God. Fasting is not a spectacle. It's not for seeking stories and experiences.

The believer who fasts and prays becomes more sensitive to conviction, more patient in trial, more dependent in decision, and more disciplined in conduct. Fasting (accompanied by prayer) is extremely useful when there are strongholds, addictions, and sinful habits. Remember, the disciples couldn't cast out a particular demonic spirit without prayer AND FASTING.

The outwards result may vary. The inward transformation is the true reward.

A Necessary Guardrail

As fasting deepens prayer life, spiritual experiences may increase. Clarity may sharpen. Conviction may intensify. But discernment becomes essential. However, not every impression is divine. Not every thought is revelation. And not every experience is from God.

In the next chapter, we will address one of the most important safeguards in spiritual disciplines: How to discern true spiritual experiences from emotional, psychological, or deceptive influences. Because discipline without discernment can lead to imbalance.

CHAPTER REVIEW

This chapter highlights the close partnership between prayer and fasting. While fasting disciplines the body, prayer directs the heart toward God. When practiced together, they create spiritual focus and intentional dependence upon the Lord. Without prayer, fasting becomes merely physical deprivation. Without discipline, prayer often becomes distracted. Together they strengthen spiritual attentiveness and deepen communion with God.

KEY SCRIPTURES

- Matthew 6:16–18
- Acts 13:2–3
- Ezra 8:21–23
- Nehemiah 1:4
- Luke 2:37

DISCUSSION QUESTIONS

(For Groups)

1. Why do Scripture passages often connect prayer with fasting?
2. How does fasting strengthen a believer's prayer life?
3. What dangers arise when fasting occurs without prayer?
4. How can believers develop deeper focus during times of prayer?

PERSONAL REFLECTION

1. How would you describe your current prayer life?

____

____

____

____

2. How might fasting help remove distractions from your time with God?

____

____

____

____

3. What specific prayer burdens might lead you to consider fasting?

____

____

____

____

JOURNAL BEFORE THE LORD

Write your prayer, reflections, and commitments below.

Anthony V. Johnson

PART III

GUARDRAILS AND ISCERNMENT

CHAPTER SIX

Discerning True Spiritual Experiences vs. Deception

Fasting increases sensitivity. As the body weakens and distractions diminish, many believers report heightened awareness — stronger impressions, deeper conviction, unusual dreams, or intensified spiritual focus.

But increased sensitivity requires increased discernment. Not every experience is divine. Not every impression is revelation. Not every spiritual sensation is from God.

Scripture commands:

"Beloved, believe not every spirit, but try the spirits whether they are of God..." (1 John 4:1)

If fasting sharpens awareness, it must also sharpen judgment.

The Danger of Misinterpretation

When the body is deprived of food, several things occur physically:

- Blood sugar levels shift.
- Sleep patterns may change.
- Emotions can intensify.
- Thoughts may feel more vivid.

Some believers mistake physiological changes for spiritual manifestations. Physical weakness can amplify imagination. And fatigue can blur emotional boundaries. This does not mean fasting is unsafe. It means fasting must be approached with sobriety.

Spiritual maturity requires the ability to distinguish between: emotional intensity, psychological reaction, genuine conviction, and divine prompting.

The Primary Test: Scripture

The Word of God is the final authority. Any impression, vision, dream, or internal prompting must be measured against Scripture. God will never contradict His Word.

If an experience contradicts Scripture, results in pride, isolation from accountability or disobedience to biblical principles, it is not from God.

The Bereans were commended in Acts 17 because they searched the Scriptures daily to confirm what they heard. Probably today more than ever before people need to search the Scriptures to know the Word for themselves.

The Fruit Test

Jesus said:

"Ye shall know them by their fruits." (Matthew 7:16)

Spiritual authenticity is revealed over time by fruit. The fruit of the Spirit includes:

- Love
- Joy
- Peace
- Longsuffering
- Gentleness
- Goodness

- Faith
- Meekness
- Temperance (Galatians 5:22–23)

If fasting produces:

- Arrogance

- Harshness

- Superiority

- Instability

- Impulsiveness

Something is misaligned. True spiritual growth increases humility. It does not inflate ego.

The Role of Accountability

One of the most dangerous environments for deception is isolation. Throughout Scripture, even strong leaders operated within community. Paul submitted his revelation to the apostles (Galatians 2). And the early church discerned together (Acts 13).

If fasting leads someone to withdraw from wise counsel, reject correction, or dismiss accountability, caution is required. Mature believers welcome confirmation. They don't demand unquestioned acceptance. Spiritual experiences that cannot withstand scriptural and pastoral examination should not be trusted.

The Subtlety of Pride

Spiritual disciplines can create spiritual pride if the heart is not guarded. It is possible to think: "I fast more than others." "I pray more deeply." "I hear God more clearly." This was the error of the Pharisee in Luke 18 when they boasted, "I fast twice in the week…" He listed his disciplines as credentials, yet he left unjustified.

The tax collector, who simply cried for mercy, left justified. Fasting that produces superiority defeats its own purpose. Fasting is meant to humble — not elevate.

Emotional Intensity vs. Spiritual Depth

During fasting, emotions may surface. You may find that tears may come easily. Conviction may feel stronger, and dreams may become vivid. There is nothing wrong with emotional intensity. But emotion alone is not proof of divine activity. Spiritual depth is measured by transformation over time — not intensity in a moment.

True spiritual encounters: strengthen obedience, increase love, produce patience, and deepens reverence for God. They do not merely create dramatic stories.

The Enemy's Counterfeit

Scripture makes clear that deception exists. Satan can appear as "an angel of light" (2 Corinthians 11:14). For more on Satan's deception, I discuss this in depth in my book "PSYOPS: The Spiritual Battle for Your Mind and Your Soul!"

The enemy exploits: physical weakness, emotional vulnerability, and spiritual zeal without knowledge. This is why fasting must never be detached from Scripture and prayer. The safest environment for spiritual growth includes:

- Biblical grounding
- Humble posture
- Wise counsel
- Balanced discipline

Spiritual warfare is real, but paranoia is not spiritual maturity. Sobriety is required.

Testing Internal Promptings

When fasting, believers may sense internal impressions. To test an impression, ask yourself:

1. Does this align with Scripture?

2. Does it produce humility?

3. Does it increase love?

4. Does it require obedience consistent with God's character?

5. Would I submit this to mature counsel?

If the answer to these questions reveals contradiction, confusion, or self-exaltation, the impression should be discarded. God is not the author of confusion (1 Corinthians 14:33).

Physical Safety and Spiritual Balance

Extended fasting without wisdom can create physical distress. Physical distress can influence perception. Consulting a physician when necessary is not lack of faith — it is stewardship. Ignoring health is not spirituality. The body is the temple of the Holy Spirit. Discernment includes knowing one's limits.

When Silence Is Better Than Interpretation

Sometimes, during fasting, unusual experiences occur. It is not always necessary to interpret immediately. Silence and patience often bring clarity. Daniel received visions — but often did not immediately understand them. Interpretation sometimes unfolded later. Not every experience requires public declaration. And maturity includes restraint.

Stability Is a Sign of Strength

Spiritual growth produces steadiness. The believer who fasts and prays should become more grounded, more patient, more measured, and more compassionate.

If fasting produces instability, something is wrong. True encounters with God produce reverence, not recklessness.

Why Discernment Matters Before Experience

It is easier to build discernment before experiences increase than to correct imbalance afterward. This chapter serves as a guardrail. Fasting can open spiritual sensitivity. Discernment ensures that sensitivity is guided by truth. Without discernment, zeal can outrun wisdom. With discernment, discipline becomes safe and fruitful.

The Foundation of Safety

The safest believer is not the one with the most experiences. It is the one who remains anchored in Scripture, in addition to humility, community, obedience and reverence. Fasting should deepen stability, not diminish it.

Transition

Now that we have established guardrails for spiritual discernment, we must address another necessary truth, the misuse associated with fasting. Throughout history, fasting has, at times, been distorted, exaggerated, weaponized, and misunderstood.

In the next chapter, we will examine common mistakes and spiritual abuses related to fasting so that this discipline remains pure and healthy.

CHAPTER REVIEW

This chapter addresses the importance of discernment during times of fasting. Because fasting can heighten spiritual sensitivity, believers must remain anchored in Scripture and guided by humility. Not every impression or experience is divine. Discernment protects the believer from confusion, deception, or spiritual imbalance and ensures that spiritual experiences remain rooted in biblical truth.

KEY SCRIPTURES

- 1 John 4:1
- Hebrews 5:14
- 2 Corinthians 11:14
- Proverbs 3:5–6
- James 1:5

DISCUSSION QUESTIONS

(For Groups)

1. Why does increased spiritual sensitivity require increased discernment?
2. What safeguards help believers evaluate spiritual experiences wisely?
3. How can Scripture help distinguish truth from deception?
4. Why is humility essential when discussing spiritual experiences?

PERSONAL REFLECTION

1. How do you normally test spiritual impressions or experiences?

____

____

____

____

2. What role does Scripture play in guiding your spiritual discernment?

____

____

____

3. How can humility protect believers from spiritual deception?

____

____

____

JOURNAL BEFORE THE LORD

Write your prayer, reflections, and commitments below.

CHAPTER SEVEN

Common Mistakes and Spiritual Abuses of Fasting

Every spiritual discipline given by God can be misused by man. Prayer can become performance, and worship can become entertainment. Teaching can become pride. And fasting can become distorted.

When fasting is misunderstood or misapplied, it can drift from consecration into extremism, legalism, manipulation, or spiritual pride.

To preserve the purity of this discipline, we must identify common mistakes and abuses — not to discourage fasting, but to guard it.

Mistake #1: Fasting to Impress Others

Jesus addressed this directly in Matthew 6:

"When ye fast, be not, as the hypocrites, of a sad countenance…"

The Pharisees intentionally altered their appearance so others would notice their sacrifice. They wanted recognition, admiration and a reputation for being spiritual.

Jesus said:

"They have their reward."

When fasting becomes public performance, its spiritual value evaporates. True fasting is directed toward God — not toward observers. The discipline loses its power when it seeks applause.

Mistake #2: Treating Fasting as a Bargaining Tool

Some approach fasting as negotiation. "If I fast long enough, God must respond." Or
"If I sacrifice more, I deserve the answers that I am seeking." This is subtle manipulation. Fasting does not twist God's arm or purchase favor. God responds to humility.

Isaiah 58 rebukes those who fasted while expecting automatic blessing, "Wherefore have we fasted… and thou seest not?" Their hearts remained unchanged, yet they expected results.

Fasting aligns the believer with God's will. It does not force God to align with ours.

Mistake #3: Legalism and Spiritual Superiority

Spiritual disciplines can easily become measurements of worth. If you say something such as, "I fast twice a week." "I do extended fasts." Or "I am more disciplined." This mindset resembles the Pharisee in Luke 18 who boasted of his fasting while despising the tax collector.

Fasting was meant to bring about humility. But when it becomes comparison, it produces pride. Legalism creeps in when believers impose personal fasting patterns on others or suggest spiritual inferiority for those who fast differently.

It is improper to measure maturity by duration rather than fruit. Maturity is revealed by love, obedience, and character — not by endurance.

Mistake #4: Ignoring Health and Wisdom

Some believers believe that enduring extreme physical distress proves greater spirituality. But Scripture never promotes recklessness. The body is a stewardship. Consulting a physician when needed does not indicate a lack of faith. We must use wisdom. God is the healer and He can use physicians for His purpose. Ignoring medical conditions is not spiritual bravery. Fasting must be approached responsibly.

When it comes to fasting, wisdom includes understanding personal health limitations. We should begin gradually, break the fast carefully, and avoid unnecessary harm. God does not require self-destruction to demonstrate devotion.

Mistake #5: Substituting Fasting for Obedience

It is possible to fast intensely while remaining disobedient. Isaiah 58 exposes this clearly. The people fasted yet they continued in injustice, wickedness and exploited others.

God declared: "Is not this the fast that I have chosen?"

Fasting cannot compensate for disobedience. If a believer fasts but refuses to forgive, refuses to repent, or refuses to obey Scripture, the fast is hollow. Obedience is always superior to sacrifice.

Mistake #6: Emotionalism Without Transformation

Some equate dramatic emotion with spiritual depth: tears, intensity or public declarations. Emotion is not wrong but it is not proof.

If fasting produces intense moments but no lasting change, it has not achieved its purpose. Fasting, if done properly, produces patience, self-control, humility and integrity. Transformation over time matters more than intensity in a moment.

Mistake #7: Extremism and Isolation

Throughout church history, some have embraced extreme asceticism believing deprivation itself results in greater holiness. But isolation without accountability is dangerous. The believer risks imbalance if there is a withdrawal from Scripture, church community or wise counsel under the banner of fasting.

The New Testament pattern emphasizes community and mutual submission. Spiritual growth flourishes in accountability not isolation.

Mistake #8: Over-Spiritualizing Every Difficulty

During fasting, normal physical symptoms may occur including headaches, fatigue and mood fluctuations. And some misinterpret discomforts as spiritual warfare.

Not every challenge is demonic resistance. Sometimes the body is simply adjusting. Discernment is essential. By over-spiritualizing ordinary experiences, you stand the risk of becoming unstable. Spiritual maturity remains calm, grounded, and scriptural.

Mistake #9: Treating Fasting as a Crisis-Only Tool

Some believers only fast during emergencies. Now, as seen in Scripture, many examples of fasting did occur in times of crisis. However, Jesus fasted for forty days and nights when there was no crisis situation. While fasting during crisis is biblical, reducing it to crisis management limits its purpose.

Fasting is not merely for emergencies, heath problems or urgent decisions. One should also fast for regular consecration, spiritual clarity, and ongoing discipline.

When fasting is used only as a last resort, it becomes reactionary rather than formative.

Mistake #10: Seeking Experiences Over Intimacy

Fasting can heighten spiritual awareness. But the goal should not be experiencing visions, manifestations, stories or supernatural experiences, although these can result from fasting. Otherwise, if you make these experiences the goal of your fast, your heart may drift.

The goal is intimacy with God. Experiences, if they occur, are secondary. When experience becomes the pursuit, deception becomes more likely. When intimacy becomes the pursuit, stability increases.

The Right Posture

The proper posture for fasting is simple: humility, dependence, and surrender to God. Fasting is not for performance, manipulation or comparison. The believer who fasts rightly does not announce it loudly. The believer simply draws near to God.

A Healthy Summary

Biblical fasting is:

- private before it is public.

- humble rather than dramatic.

- obedient rather than performative.

- scriptural rather than sensational.

- balanced rather than extreme.

It strengthens character, refines motives, and deepens reverence.

Guarding the Discipline

Fasting is powerful, but power without guardrails leads to harm. By recognizing common abuses, we protect the integrity of the practice. We also protect ourselves.

The goal is not to frighten believers away from fasting. The goal is to ensure that when they fast, they do so safely, wisely, and biblically.

Transition

Fasting, when practiced correctly, strengthens spiritual awareness. And with strengthened awareness comes confrontation.

Spiritual resistance may increase. Temptation may intensify. Battles that were subtle may become obvious.

In the next chapter, we will examine the relationship between fasting and spiritual warfare — and how discipline prepares the believer for unseen conflict.

CHAPTER REVIEW

This chapter explores common distortions of fasting that occur when spiritual disciplines are misunderstood. When fasting becomes a source of pride, legalism, or manipulation, it loses its intended purpose. Biblical fasting calls believers to humility, sincerity, and obedience—not spiritual performance. Recognizing these dangers helps believers practice fasting responsibly.

KEY SCRIPTURES

- Matthew 6:16–18
- Luke 18:10–14
- Isaiah 58:3–5
- Colossians 2:20–23
- Micah 6:8

DISCUSSION QUESTIONS

(For Groups)

1. What examples of spiritual pride or misuse of fasting have you observed?
2. Why can spiritual disciplines become distorted over time?
3. How can churches teach fasting while guarding against legalism?
4. What attitudes help maintain humility in spiritual disciplines?

PERSONAL REFLECTION

1. Are there areas where spiritual discipline could become prideful or performative?

____

____

____

____

2. What motivations should guide fasting in the life of a believer?

____

____

____

3. How can you pursue fasting in a way that remains humble and sincere?

____

____

____

JOURNAL BEFORE THE LORD

Write your prayer, reflections, and commitments below.

CHAPTER EIGHT

Fasting and Spiritual Warfare

The Bible does not deny the existence of spiritual conflict. It reveals it.

From Genesis to Revelation, Scripture affirms that there is more occurring than what is visible to the natural eye. The believer lives not only in a physical world, but in a spiritual one.

Paul writes:

"For we wrestle not against flesh and blood, but against principalities, against powers, against the rulers of the darkness of this world…" (Ephesians 6:12)

Spiritual warfare is not imaginary. But neither is it theatrical. It is real and often subtle. Fasting intersects with spiritual warfare not because it is mystical, but because it strengthens alignment.

The Foundation of Warfare: Submission

Before Scripture speaks of resisting the devil, it speaks of submission.

James 4:7 says: "Submit yourselves therefore to God. Resist the devil, and he will flee from you." Notice the order. Submission comes first. Resistance follows.

Fasting is an act of submission. It declares: "My flesh does not rule me." "My appetite does not govern me." "My will is not supreme."

Spiritual authority flows from alignment. A believer who refuses to submit to God cannot expect to resist the enemy effectively. Fasting strengthens submission, and submission strengthens authority.

Jesus in the Wilderness

Matthew 4 reveals a critical pattern. Jesus fasted forty days and forty nights. After the fast, temptation came. The wilderness was not accidental, and the confrontation was not random.

The fast did not create the enemy's presence but it preceded the encounter. And notice how Jesus responded. Jesus didn't respond with emotion, spectacle or ritual. He responded with Scripture: "It is written…"

Three times Jesus quoted the Word. The fast prepared Him, but the Word defeated the temptation. Fasting without Scripture is incomplete. Scripture without surrender is ineffective. Together, they strengthen the believer.

Why Temptation May Intensify During a Fast

Many believers report increased temptation while fasting. As you probably already know, temptation is strongest during periods of weakness. This should not surprise us.

When the body is denied its normal patterns, resistance rises. The flesh protests. Cravings intensify. Old habits attempt to resurface.

Fasting exposes what controls you. When control shifts from flesh to spirit, tension occurs. This is not evidence of failure. It is evidence of confrontation.

Galatians 5:17 reminds us: "The flesh lusteth against the Spirit…" Fasting magnifies that battle temporarily. But magnification leads to clarity. Clarity leads to victory.

Authority Through Alignment

In Mark 9, Jesus said: "This kind can come forth by nothing, but by prayer and fasting." Authority in spiritual warfare is not about volume. It is about alignment.

A believer who walks in consistent surrender, prayer, and discipline carries greater spiritual steadiness. This does not mean dramatic manifestations will always occur. It means spiritual resistance is met with stability rather than panic.

Spiritual warfare is not about shouting. It is about standing. Ephesians 6 repeatedly says: "Stand." Fasting strengthens the believer's ability to stand.

Spiritual Warfare Is Not Paranoia

It must be stated clearly, not every inconvenience is spiritual attack. Not every headache is an act of oppression. Not every difficulty is demonic resistance. An unhealthy fixation on warfare leads to imbalance.

Scripture presents spiritual warfare as reality, but it does not promote obsession. The believer's focus remains on Christ, not the enemy.

Colossians 2:15 declares that Christ has already triumphed. We fight from victory — not for victory.

Fasting is not about chasing demons. It is about strengthening devotion.

Guarding the Mind During Fasting

Because fasting can heighten sensitivity, the mind must remain guarded. Paul writes:

"Casting down imaginations…" (2 Corinthians 10:5). When fasting guard against exaggerated interpretation and fear. Guard against spiritual grandiosity and isolation.

The helmet of salvation protects the mind. Scripture stabilizes perception. And accountability protects judgment.

The Armor of God and Fasting

Ephesians 6 outlines spiritual armor: Truth, Righteousness, Peace, Faith, Salvation, and the Word of God. Notice that fasting is not listed as armor. Fasting strengthens the believer and sharpens alertness.

It disciplines the soldier. But the armor itself remains truth and righteousness. If a believer fasts without truth, imbalance follows. If a believer fasts without righteousness, hypocrisy follows. Fasting enhances readiness. It does not replace armor.

Corporate Warfare and Fasting

Throughout Scripture, there were moments when communities fasted during national crisis. In 2 Chronicles 20, Jehoshaphat proclaimed a fast when armies advanced against Judah. The people gathered and humbled themselves.

God gave direction which was followed by victory. The fast did not create military power. It positioned the nation to receive divine strategy. Corporate fasting in times of moral or cultural crisis can produce clarity and unity when rooted in repentance and obedience.

The Quiet Nature of Most Warfare

Spiritual warfare is often quieter than expected. It may look like resisting temptation, forgiving an offense, controlling anger, refusing compromise, or persisting in obedience.

Fasting strengthens discipline. Discipline strengthens resistance. Resistance strengthens character. And character strengthens endurance. Endurance silences the enemy more effectively than spectacle.

When Not to Fast

There are seasons when a believer may need nourishment more than denial. In times of illness, extreme stress, or medical vulnerability, wisdom is required.

Spiritual warfare is not about proving toughness. It is about walking wisely. God values obedience over extremism.

The Greater Victory

The greatest victory in spiritual warfare is not dramatic deliverance. It is sustained faithfulness. It is the believer who walks uprightly, controls speech, subdues pride, maintains integrity, and resists temptation quietly.

Fasting strengthens these victories. It trains the believer to say "no" to the flesh and "yes" to God.

A Final Word of Balance

Fasting is a tool not a weapon of spectacle. It is preparation not performance. It is discipline not drama. The believer who fasts biblically becomes more grounded, not more erratic, more humble, not more inflated. The believer becomes more stable, not more extreme. And that stability is one of the strongest forms of spiritual authority.

Transition

If fasting strengthens spiritual endurance and steadiness, it must not be treated as an occasional emergency tool. It must become part of a broader rhythm of discipline.

In the next chapter, we will explore how to develop a sustainable lifestyle of fasting — one that cultivates long-term spiritual maturity rather than short-term intensity.

CHAPTER REVIEW

This chapter explores the relationship between fasting and spiritual conflict. Scripture reveals that believers live in both physical and spiritual realities. While fasting does not grant magical power, it strengthens spiritual focus and dependence upon God. In times of spiritual opposition, fasting can accompany prayer as believers seek God's intervention and guidance.

KEY SCRIPTURES

- Ephesians 6:12
- Mark 9:29
- Daniel 10:12–13
- James 4:7
- 2 Corinthians 10:3–5

DISCUSSION QUESTIONS

(For Groups)

1. How does Scripture describe spiritual warfare?
2. What role might fasting play in times of spiritual conflict?
3. Why must believers avoid sensationalizing spiritual warfare?
4. How can believers remain balanced while acknowledging spiritual realities?

PERSONAL REFLECTION

1. How do you normally respond to spiritual challenges or opposition?

____

____

____

____

2. What role could prayer and fasting play in strengthening your faith during conflict?

____

____

____

____

3. How can you remain grounded in Scripture while confronting spiritual struggles?

____

____

____

JOURNAL BEFORE THE LORD

Write your prayer, reflections, and commitments below.

PART IV
A LIFESTYLE OF CONSECRATION

CHAPTER NINE

Developing a Discipline of Fasting

When it comes to fasting, it should not be impulsive. It should not be driven by emotion alone, and it should not be limited to crisis.

If fasting is treated only as an emergency response, it becomes reactionary rather than formative. But when fasting becomes part of a believer's spiritual rhythm, it produces stability, endurance, and depth.

The goal is not intensity. The goal is consistency.

From Event to Discipline

Many believers first fast during moments of desperation, for example, a health crisis, financial emergency, difficult decision or a family conflict. And these are valid moments to fast. But if fasting is only associated with emergencies, it will rarely mature into discipline.

Discipline is something practiced intentionally not occasionally. It is integrated into life. It becomes part of spiritual formation.

Just as prayer should not be reserved for crisis, fasting should not be limited to panic.

Biblical Rhythms of Fasting

Scripture does not prescribe a universal schedule for fasting, but it demonstrates patterns. The early church fasted before sending missionaries (Acts 13). Jesus assumed fasting would be part of discipleship (Matthew 6).

Some fasted during seasons of repentance. Others fasted during seasons of seeking direction. The principle is not frequency. The principle is intentionality.

A sustainable rhythm may look like:

- A one-day fast once a month, or once a week.

- A three-day fast once a month.

- A seasonal fast during specific times of reflection.

- Occasional extended fasts when led clearly and wisely.

There is freedom, but there must be wisdom.

Starting Wisely

For those new to fasting, beginning slowly is important. Sustainable discipline begins with, perhaps, skipping one meal intentionally and setting aside that time for prayer. Also, reflecting rather than rushing. Growth comes gradually. Spiritual disciplines resemble physical training. Attempting extremes too quickly can produce discouragement or harm. Building steadily creates endurance.

The Heart Behind the Discipline

A regular rhythm of fasting should never become mechanical. The believer must guard against routines lacking reflection, habits without humility, or discipline without devotion.

Each fast should include prayerful preparation and examination of motives. The fast should include Scriptural meditation and repentance where necessary.

The discipline must remain relational. Otherwise, it becomes ritual.

Integrating Fasting with Daily Life

Fasting should not disconnect believers from responsibilities. Scripture does not teach neglect of family, work, or obligations in the name of fasting.

Mature discipline means maintaining responsibilities, avoiding irritability, and continuing to serve faithfully.

If fasting makes a believer harsh, withdrawn, resentful or neglectful, balance must be restored. The fruit of the Spirit must remain evident.

Corporate and Private Balance

Private fasting builds personal depth. And corporate fasting builds unity. There may be seasons when a church calls for communal fasting, for example for repentance, clarity, or direction. But the foundation must be private discipline.

If a believer only fasts when others do, the practice remains external. Personal conviction must lead.

Avoiding Comparison

Comparison quietly undermines spiritual growth. Some fast longer. Some fast more frequently. Some cannot fast extensively due to health.

Spiritual maturity is not measured by duration. It is measured by transformation. The believer must resist the urge to compare. Discipline should produce humility — not competition.

Evaluating Growth Over Time

A sustainable fasting discipline should produce noticeable fruit over months and years. Ask yourself, "Am I more patient?" "Am I quick to repent?" "Am I less controlled by appetite?" "Am I more attentive in prayer?" And, "Am I growing in self-control?" If the answer is yes, the discipline is healthy.

An adjustment is necessary if fasting produces pride, instability, extremism or a feeling of spiritual superiority. Spiritual growth is steady not explosive.

Seasons of Intensified Consecration

There may be seasons when the Lord leads into deeper consecration. These seasons require:

- Clear purpose.

- Medical wisdom if necessary.

- Accountability.

- Scriptural grounding.

Extended fasting should not be entered lightly. It should be prayerfully discerned. The body must be respected, and the mind must remain sober. And remember, humility plays a large part when it comes to fasting. The heart must remain humble.

The Long-Term Impact

Over time, disciplined fasting strengthens self-control which is foundational to spiritual maturity. When a believer learns to say "no" to food voluntarily, it becomes easier to say "no" to temptation, anger, impatience and compromise. The discipline carries over.

Fasting builds spiritual resilience, trains the will, and stabilizes the soul. This is the quiet power of fasting.

Keeping the Discipline Hidden

Jesus emphasized secrecy for a reason. The discipline is strengthened when it remains between the believer and God.

Not every fast needs announcement. Not every discipline requires explanation.

Hidden obedience cultivates sincerity, and God who sees what is done in secret will reward you openly.

A Lifestyle of Dependence

Ultimately, fasting is about dependence on God. It is a reminder that man does not live by bread alone. Strength, direction and sustenance all come from God.

When fasting becomes a rhythm, dependence becomes natural. The believer becomes less reactive, less controlled by impulse, more anchored in conviction. And that anchoring produces stability.

Preparing for Deeper Testimony

Disciplined fasting over time produces stories. But those stories are not the goal. They are the byproduct.

When discipline is sustained, experiences may follow but they must always be interpreted through Scripture, humility, and discernment.

Fasting requires foundation. And the foundation is this: Fasting is not about intensity. It is about intimacy. It is not about spectacle, it's about surrender. It is not about proving strength. It is about embracing dependence.

In the next chapter, we will discuss common misconceptions about fasting.

CHAPTER REVIEW

This chapter encourages believers to view fasting as a regular discipline rather than an occasional reaction to crisis. When practiced consistently and wisely, fasting becomes part of a believer's spiritual rhythm. Over time, it cultivates endurance, humility, and deeper dependence upon God.

KEY SCRIPTURES

- 1 Corinthians 9:24–27
- Hebrews 12:11
- Luke 5:33–35
- 1 Timothy 4:7–8
- Psalm 63:1

DISCUSSION QUESTIONS

(For Groups)

1. Why is spiritual discipline important for long-term spiritual growth?
2. How can fasting become part of a believer's regular spiritual rhythm?
3. What obstacles make spiritual discipline difficult to maintain?
4. How can accountability help believers remain consistent?

PERSONAL REFLECTION

1. What spiritual disciplines are currently part of your routine?

____

____

____

____

2. How might fasting become a healthy rhythm in your life?

____

____

____

3. What practical steps would help you grow in spiritual discipline?

____

____

____

____

JOURNAL BEFORE THE LORD

Write your prayer, reflections, and commitments below.

CHAPTER TEN

COMMON MISCONCEPTIONS ABOUT FASTING IN MODERN CHRISTIANITY

The Need for Clarity

In every generation, biblical practices can become distorted through tradition, imbalance, or cultural adaptation. Fasting is no exception. In some circles, fasting has been neglected entirely. In others, it has been exaggerated, sensationalized, or redefined.

If fasting is to be restored to its proper place in the life of the believer and the Church, it must be understood clearly and practiced biblically.

This chapter addresses several widespread misconceptions about fasting and seeks to correct them through Scripture.

1. Fasting Is Not a Diet Plan

One of the most common distortions in modern Christianity is the merging of fasting with dieting.

"Biblical" fasting is **NOT**:

- A detox program

- A weight-loss strategy

- A metabolic reset

- A health trend

While physical benefits may occur during a fast, Scripture never presents fasting as a physical discipline for bodily improvement. It is always presented as a spiritual act of humility before God.

Isaiah 58 makes it clear that fasting without spiritual purpose is empty. God rebuked Israel not because they abstained from food, but because they fasted without righteousness, justice, or repentance.

If fasting becomes centered on physical results rather than spiritual alignment, its purpose has already been compromised.

2. The "Daniel Fast" as a Substitute for Biblical Fasting

As discussed earlier, Daniel 1 ***does not*** describe a fast. It describes dietary separation for ceremonial purity. Daniel did eat. He consumed pulse and water.

True biblical fasting, as demonstrated consistently throughout Scripture, involved ***abstaining from food entirely*** for a set period.

Daniel 9:3, however, describes an actual fast: "I set my face unto the Lord God, to seek by prayer and supplications, with fasting, and sackcloth, and ashes."

The modern adaptation known as the "Daniel Fast" is often a well-intentioned dietary discipline. But it should not be equated with the "biblical fast" described in Scripture.

Precision matters. Stick to the Word of God not traditions of men.

3. Fasting Does Not Manipulate God

Another dangerous misconception is the idea that fasting forces God to act. Fasting is not leverage. It is not a bargaining chip, and it is not a spiritual currency.

In Isaiah 58, Israel essentially asked, "Why have we fasted, and You have not seen?" God's response revealed that their fasting was self-centered. Fasting does not twist the arm of God. It humbles the heart of man.

When Nineveh fasted, God responded not because they manipulated Him, but because they genuinely repented. The posture of the heart determines the response of God.

4. Fasting Is Not Spiritual Pride

Jesus addressed this directly in Matthew 6:16–18. He warned against fasting "to be seen of men." Spiritual disciplines can become vehicles for pride if not guarded.

Fasting does not make one superior or elevate one above others. There is no spiritual hierarchy that is created because of fasting.

The Pharisees fasted twice weekly (Luke 18:12), yet Jesus commended the humble tax collector who cried for mercy.

Fasting without humility becomes self-righteousness. True fasting increases dependence not ego.

5. Fasting Is Not Emotionalism

Some equate fasting with intense emotional experiences. While fasting may heighten spiritual sensitivity, it is not primarily about feelings. It is about alignment.

Scripture never commands believers to chase experiences. It calls them to seek God.

If emotional manifestations occur, they must be evaluated through Scripture and spiritual discernment.

The Word of God remains the standard — not sensations.

6. Western Comfort Culture and the Loss of Fasting

In much of Western Christianity, fasting has quietly disappeared. Why? Because fasting confronts comfort. Modern culture, especially in the West, values convenience and seeks to avoid discomfort. Personal satisfaction is prioritized. Fasting contradicts these values.

Fasting denies appetite, rejects indulgence and embraces restraint.

The early Church fasted regularly (Acts 13:2–3; Acts 14:23).

Today, many churches rarely mention fasting. The decline of fasting may correlate with the decline of spiritual authority and discernment. Have you observed what is currently taking place in many ministries across nations? This is not condemnation. It is observation. Restoring fasting restores discipline.

7. Fasting and Legalism

Some believers avoid fasting because they associate it with legalism. Legalism says:

"If I fast, God owes me." Biblical fasting says: "I fast because I need Him." Legalism focuses on performance. Biblical fasting focuses on humility.

When practiced properly, fasting increases grace-awareness, not religious pressure.

8. Fasting and Spiritual Warfare Obsession

While Mark 9:29 reveals that certain spiritual breakthroughs are connected to prayer and fasting, fasting should not become an obsession with demonic confrontation. The focus of fasting is God — not demons.

When attention shifts excessively toward spiritual enemies, imbalance occurs. The believer fasts to seek God, not to hunt darkness. Light naturally dispels darkness.

Fasting must be reclaimed — not reinvented. It must be grounded in Scripture, guarded by humility, and practiced with wisdom.

When misconceptions are removed, fasting becomes what God intended: A sacred discipline of alignment, repentance, clarity, and power.

CHAPTER REVIEW

This chapter addresses common misunderstandings about fasting within modern Christianity. Cultural influences, traditions, and misinformation have often reshaped how fasting is viewed. Returning to Scripture allows believers to rediscover fasting as a balanced, meaningful practice rooted in humility and devotion.

KEY SCRIPTURES

- Matthew 6:16–18
- Isaiah 58:3–7
- Colossians 2:8
- Romans 12:2
- Psalm 119:105

DISCUSSION QUESTIONS

(For Groups)

1. What misconceptions about fasting have you encountered in modern Christianity?
2. Why do biblical practices often become distorted over time?
3. How can believers return to a balanced understanding of fasting?
4. Why is Scripture the ultimate guide for spiritual practices?

PERSONAL REFLECTION

1. What assumptions about fasting have you held in the past?

2. How has Scripture reshaped your understanding of fasting?

3. What changes might God be prompting in your spiritual life?

JOURNAL BEFORE THE LORD

Write your prayer, reflections, and commitments below.

CHAPTER ELEVEN

FASTING IN REDEMPTIVE HISTORY

To understand fasting fully, we must trace its place throughout the unfolding story of redemption.

Fasting did not begin with the Church. It did not originate with Jesus' ministry. It was woven throughout God's dealings with His people.

This chapter examines fasting across biblical history.

1. Fasting Under the Law

The Day of Atonement (Leviticus 16:29–31) required Israel to "afflict their souls," widely understood to include fasting. This was not optional. It was national.

The purpose? Repentance. Atonement. Humility before God.

Fasting was embedded into covenant life.

2. Fasting in Times of National Crisis

Throughout the Historical Books, fasting appears during:

- War (Judges 20:26)

- National defeat (1 Samuel 7:6)

- Mourning (2 Samuel 1:12)

- Judgment warnings (1 Kings 21:27)

Fasting marked moments of desperation and dependence. It acknowledged that human strength was insufficient.

3. Fasting During Exile and Restoration

Ezra, Nehemiah, and Daniel fasted during periods of rebuilding and repentance. Daniel 9 connects fasting directly with prophetic revelation. Nehemiah 1 links fasting with intercession for national restoration. Fasting became a vehicle of confession and rebuilding.

4. Prophetic Calls to Fasting

The prophets repeatedly called Israel to fasting, not ritualistically, but sincerely.

In Joel 2:12, the Scripture says, "Turn ye even to me with all your heart, and with fasting…" Isaiah 58 corrected empty fasting. Zechariah 7:5 questioned the motive behind fasting. And the prophets consistently emphasized heart alignment over outward action.

5. Fasting in the Ministry of Christ

Jesus fasted forty days (Matthew 4:1–2). He taught about fasting (Matthew 6). He assumed His disciples would fast: "When ye fast…" (not if).

He declared that after His departure, His followers would fast (Matthew 9:15).

Fasting was not abolished in the New Covenant. It was assumed.

6. Fasting in the Early Church

In Acts 13:2–3 the Church fasted before sending Paul and Barnabas. In Acts 14:23

Elders were appointed with prayer and fasting. Fasting was connected to: leadership selection, mission commissioning, and spiritual direction. It was not fringe. It was foundational.

7. Fasting in Church History

The Didache (1st–2nd century) instructed believers to fast regularly. Early Christians fasted twice weekly. John Wesley fasted regularly and expected Methodist leaders to do the same.

Throughout history, spiritual awakenings were often preceded by seasons of prayer and fasting.

Over time, however, fasting declined in prominence. Modern Christianity retained preaching, music, and programs but often lost discipline.

8. Theological Significance

Across redemptive history, fasting consistently represents:

- Humility before God
- Dependence on God
- Repentance
- Spiritual preparation
- Seeking direction
- Intensified intercession

It was never casual or recreational. It was never trendy. It was sacred. From Moses to the prophets…From Christ to the early Church…From revival movements to faithful believers across centuries…Fasting has always accompanied serious pursuit of God.

When properly understood, fasting is not extreme. It is historical. It is biblical. It is covenantal. And it remains relevant today.

CHAPTER REVIEW

This chapter traces fasting throughout the story of redemption in Scripture. From the Old Testament to the early church, fasting appears repeatedly in the lives of God's people. These examples demonstrate that fasting has always been part of the believer's pursuit of God and remains relevant today.

KEY SCRIPTURES

- Exodus 34:28
- Nehemiah 1:4
- Daniel 9:3
- Acts 13:2–3
- Luke 4:1–2

DISCUSSION QUESTIONS

(For Groups)

1. What patterns of fasting appear throughout biblical history?
2. How did fasting shape the lives of God's people in different eras?
3. Why is it important to study spiritual disciplines in their historical context?
4. What lessons can modern believers learn from these examples?

PERSONAL REFLECTION

1. How does seeing fasting across biblical history affect your perspective on it?

____

____

____

____

2. What example of fasting in Scripture speaks most strongly to you?

____

____

____

____

3. How might you respond to God's invitation to seek Him more deeply?

____

____

____

JOURNAL BEFORE THE LORD

Write your prayer, reflections, and commitments below.

____

____

____

____

____

____

____

____

____

____

____

CHAPTER TWELVE

FASTING AS A REGULAR DISCIPLINE IN THE CHRISTIAN LIFE

Not Occasional, But Intentional

Fasting should not be treated as an emergency button that is pressed only during crisis. Nor should it be reserved exclusively for extreme spiritual moments.

Throughout Scripture, fasting appears not only in times of desperation, but also as a regular expression of devotion. The modern believer often asks, "How often should I fast?" That question reveals something important. We instinctively know fasting belongs in the life of faith, but we are uncertain how it fits.

This chapter addresses both the necessity and the rhythm of fasting in the Christian walk.

1. Jesus Assumed His Followers Would Fast

In Matthew 6:16, Jesus did not say, "If you fast." He said: "When ye fast…" That single word carries weight. Just as He said: "When you give…" "When you pray…" Fasting was assumed.

Later, in Matthew 9:15, Jesus declared: "The days will come, when the bridegroom shall be taken from them, and then shall they fast." We are living in those days.

The early Church understood this. Fasting was woven into their corporate and personal devotion. If prayer remains relevant, fasting remains relevant.

2. Fasting as Spiritual Maintenance, Not Just Emergency Response

As previously discussed, many believers fast only when facing a crisis or in need of an answer or clarity. Believers also tend to fast when facing intense spiritual warfare. While fasting during crisis is biblical, it is not the only purpose.

Regular fasting maintains spiritual sensitivity, prevents fleshly dominance, cultivates humility, and strengthens discipline.

Just as physical exercise strengthens the body gradually, fasting strengthens the spirit progressively.

Without discipline, spiritual dullness sets in. And without periodic self-denial, appetite quietly takes control. Fasting recalibrates the believer.

3. The Danger of Irregular Discipline

If fasting is absent from the Christian life entirely, several consequences may emerge, increased dependency on comfort, decreased sensitivity to conviction, heightened susceptibility to temptation, and reduced spiritual clarity. The flesh does not weaken on its own. It grows stronger when fed continually.

Paul wrote in 1 Corinthians 9:27: "I keep under my body, and bring it into subjection..." That language implies intentional discipline. Fasting is one expression of that discipline.

4. How Often Should a Christian Fast?

Scripture does not mandate universal frequency. However, history and biblical precedent give guidance.

Biblical Patterns

- The Pharisees fasted twice weekly (Luke 18:12) — though often for wrong reasons.
- The early Church fasted regularly (Acts 13; Acts 14).
- The Didache instructed believers to fast twice weekly.

While legalistic repetition is not the goal, rhythm is beneficial.

A Balanced Recommendation

For most believers, a healthy rhythm may include: fasting at least once per month for three days. If you prefer to fast in 24-hour increments, maybe fasting one full day per week may suffice. Remember, during your time of fasting, completely abstain from eating food.

Extended fasts during specific seasons of seeking God are also beneficial. Jesus went on an extended fast before He performed ANY miracles. However, frequency should grow gradually. Wisdom must guide duration, and health considerations must be respected.

Fasting should never be competitive or extreme for appearance. It should be sustainable.

5. Corporate Fasting

Throughout Scripture, entire communities fasted together: Nineveh, Israel, the early church, etc., corporate fasting unifies hearts, aligns congregations, prepares churches for breakthrough, and seeks collective repentance.

Churches that restore corporate prayer and fasting often rediscover spiritual depth. This may explain why many revival movements historically included coordinated seasons of prayer and fasting.

6. Guarding Against Burnout and Extremism

If fasting becomes excessive or constant without wisdom, imbalance occurs. Symptoms of imbalance may include physical exhaustion, spiritual pride, emotional instability, or obsession with spiritual manifestations.

Fasting must be paired with Scripture, appropriate rest, accountability and medical wisdom when necessary.

The goal is strength not depletion.

7. Fasting and Maturity

Hebrews 5:14 says: "Strong meat belongeth to them that are of full age…" Spiritual maturity requires discipline. Just as children crave sweets, immature believers often resist denial. As believers grow, they increasingly value what strengthens the spirit more than what satisfies the flesh.

Fasting becomes less intimidating and more natural. Fasting is not enjoyable in the flesh but is meaningful in the spirit.

8. A Lifelong Perspective

Fasting should not be viewed as a one-time spiritual event, a seasonal novelty, or a dramatic display. It is a lifelong companion to prayer.

Some seasons may require additional fasting. Other seasons may require maintenance fasting. The key is sensitivity to the Holy Spirit.

Fasting is not an extreme practice reserved for prophets. And it is not optional spirituality for the overly devoted. It is a biblical discipline that strengthens the believer's walk. The question is not merely "How often should I fast?" The better question is: "How serious am I about spiritual growth?"

When practiced wisely and regularly, fasting becomes: A reset for the soul, a guard against spiritual drift, a tool for humility, and a catalyst for clarity. Fasting should be consistent, intentional and personal.

In my final chapter I will share a few of my personal experiences from an extended fast, but you will find my full testimony in my upcoming book "Step Into The Supernatural" which combines fasting and praying in the spirit.

CHAPTER REVIEW

This chapter emphasizes that fasting should not be treated merely as a reaction to crisis but as a regular discipline within the Christian life. Throughout Scripture, fasting appears not only during emergencies but also as a deliberate expression of devotion and spiritual attentiveness.

When practiced wisely, fasting becomes part of a believer's spiritual rhythm—much like prayer, study of Scripture, and worship. Rather than being driven by urgency or emotion, intentional fasting cultivates humility, strengthens spiritual endurance, and deepens dependence upon God. By integrating fasting into a consistent spiritual life, believers grow in maturity and develop greater sensitivity to the leading of the Holy Spirit.

KEY SCRIPTURES

- Luke 5:33–35
- Acts 13:2–3
- Acts 14:23
- 1 Corinthians 9:24–27
- Psalm 63:1

DISCUSSION QUESTIONS

(For Groups)

1. Why is it important to view fasting as a regular spiritual discipline rather than only a response to crisis?
2. What challenges might believers face when trying to incorporate fasting into a consistent spiritual routine?

3. How can churches or small groups encourage healthy and balanced practices of fasting?
4. In what ways can regular spiritual disciplines, including fasting—strengthen long-term spiritual growth?

PERSONAL REFLECTION

1. How have you previously approached fasting—primarily during crisis, or as a regular practice of devotion?

____

____

____

____

2. What practical steps could help you incorporate fasting into a balanced and sustainable spiritual routine?

____

____

____

3. How might consistent spiritual disciplines deepen your dependence on God and strengthen your walk of faith?

____

____

____

____

JOURNAL BEFORE THE LORD

Write your prayer, reflections, and commitments below.

CHAPTER THIRTEEN

WHEN FASTING MEETS THE SUPERNATURAL: (My Experience)

My journey of extended fasting began when God placed me in a position where I had to call upon Him for my everyday needs. I have often referred to this period as a "forced fast."

The circumstances leading to this extended fasting period began when I arrived at law school with four hundred dollars in my pocket, no income, and no place to stay. My prayers began in earnest. I needed a place to stay. God opened a door, and I received free housing for six months.

It did not take long for the four hundred dollars to run out. Each law book cost three hundred dollars or more. Yet God made a way for me to purchase the books that I needed.

The school was a Catholic institution, and there was a nun who held what she called "Scripture Reflections" on Friday mornings at 10:00. I began regularly attending the Scripture Reflections and assisting the nun.

With no money, the extended fasting period had begun. I would literally go weeks without eating, yet I continued attending the Scripture Reflections—telling no one about my situation.

I began listening to a pastor's five-minute radio broadcast and eventually decided to visit his church. Shortly after I began attending, I was sitting in the sanctuary one day when I heard a voice in my spirit say, "It's time." Immediately after I heard those words, the bishop's wife asked, "Who in here knows how to play an instrument?"

I raised my hand, and she called me forward.

"What kind of instrument do you play?" she asked.

"The drums," I replied.

She said, "Go get on the drums!"

From that moment, I became a member of the worship team.

As the extended fast continued, an urgent call went out to the church members for an emergency meeting. When I arrived at the church, the bishop's wife was visibly distressed. She informed the congregation that the bishop had used their personal residence as collateral to purchase the church building, and now the creditors were threatening to seize both their home and the church property.

Various people began raising their hands and offering suggestions. I then raised my hand and said, "I think what the church needs is prayer and fasting."

She responded, "I think Anthony is right. Everyone come to the altar and pray."

When I suggested prayer and fasting, I had been thinking about prayer and fasting over a period of time. I was not expecting to be called to pray immediately. Nevertheless, I went to the altar, knelt, and began praying in the Spirit. No words were spoken in English.

After about ten to fifteen minutes of praying in the Spirit, I felt led to ask the pastor for a Bible. He ran to his office, grabbed his Bible, and brought it back to me. I had absolutely no idea what was about to take place.

The Lord instructed me to turn to a particular book and chapter in the Bible. I did not know what the passage said, but

I began reading it aloud before the entire congregation. Then the Lord said, "Stop there."

To the amazement of everyone present—including me—the passage I had just read directly addressed the situation the bishop was facing.

The pastor then walked over to me, placed his hand on my head, and said, "I ordain you a prophet…a seer."

From that moment forward, I began operating in that office.

The extended fast continued into the second year, with occasional breaks.

One afternoon I was in my apartment facing imminent eviction. I had no money and no food. I was standing in the living room, and the room was completely silent. Suddenly an extremely heavy anointing came upon me. It was very intense. I felt an overwhelming desire to dance before the Lord with all my might.

I immediately sensed that it was the spirit of David.

The Scripture says in 2 Samuel 6:14:

"And David danced before the LORD with all his might; and David was girded with a linen ephod."

I was startled, but I knew that David was the only reference in Scripture associated with such an expression. The fact that it was the spirit of David was later confirmed on multiple occasions.

There are several Scriptures in which an anointing or spirit was transferred. The most notable example is the spirit transferred from Elijah to Elisha.

The Scripture says in 2 Kings 2:9:

"And it came to pass, when they were gone over, that Elijah said unto Elisha, Ask what I shall do for thee, before I be taken away from thee. And Elisha said, I pray thee, let a double portion of thy spirit be upon me. And he said, Thou hast asked a hard thing: nevertheless, if thou see me when I am taken from thee, it shall be so unto thee…"

Other passages also reflect the transfer of spiritual anointing: Moses to the seventy elders (Numbers 11:17), Moses to Joshua (Numbers 27:18–23), and Paul and the early church (Acts 19:1–6).

As further confirmation, the Lord gave me three dreams, two of which involved spiritual warfare.

In the first dream, I was engaged in battle with a demonic spirit. I struck the demon with a rock, and it immediately blinded and paralyzed from the waist down.

In the second dream, I struck a demonic figure in the forehead with a rock, and the demon disintegrated into a pile of dust.

David slew Goliath with a stone. The Scripture says in 1 Samuel 17:49:

"And David put his hand in his bag, and took thence a stone, and slung it, and smote the Philistine in his forehead…"

In a third dream, I was walking with a pastor on a hill. In front of us stood a gazebo. Along the top of the structure were alternating heads of lions and bears. In the dream I knew immediately that the lion and the bear were references to David.

The Scripture says in 1 Samuel 17:34–36:

"Thy servant slew both the lion and the bear…"

On another occasion, I visited a church where the drummer was absent. The worship leader was pressing into prophetic worship. I asked the elder if I could play the drums. He gave me permission, and we began worshiping the Lord.

As the anointing increased, I began prophesying while playing the drums.

The Scripture says in 1 Chronicles 25:1:

"Moreover, David and the captains of the host separated to the service of the sons of Asaph…who should prophesy with harps, with psalteries, and with cymbals."

When I finished playing, I threw my drumsticks down in front of the altar. When a woman went to pick them up, she was immediately struck by the power of God.

The pastor then said to me, "Something you played on the drums…something you just played. There was a demonic spirit at a business two doors down. Something you just played…the demon left and will never come back."

The Scripture says in 1 Samuel 16:23:

"And it came to pass, when the evil spirit…was upon Saul, that David took an harp, and played with his hand… and the evil spirit departed from him."

The final confirmation occurred while I was meeting with several pastors and their wives. As we concluded our meeting, I prayed the closing prayer. One of the ministers said to me, "It was nice meeting you, David."

I asked her, "Why did you call me David?"

She replied, "I didn't call you David. The Holy Spirit called you David."

There are far too many encounters that occurred during my extended fast to include here, but I will close this chapter with the following experiences.

Many years earlier, when I first began seeking the Lord, I was walking down a street in San Francisco when the Lord told me in my spirit that He wanted me to attend a Bible school somewhere in the Oakland area. I resisted immediately because I did not want to be a pastor.

After the extended fast, unusual encounters began occurring.

One day I was walking to the restroom in a restaurant when a Hispanic woman approached me and said, "You're a pastor, aren't you?"

"No," I replied.

She looked at me with a puzzled expression.

On another occasion, I was entering an entertainment venue at Disney World in Florida. Two men were working at the door, and one of them said, "You look like a pastor!"

Similarly, while dressed in a sweatsuit, I went to a Chick-fil-A to pick up food. When the elderly man handed me my order, he said, "Here you go, pastor."

After recovering from my first bout with COVID, I visited a doctor. He walked into the room, looked at his clipboard, and said, "You're a pastor, aren't you?"

When I replied "No", he said, "Hmm. For some reason I thought you were a pastor. You missed your calling."

On another day I was walking across a parking lot when an elderly man pushing a garbage container shouted, "Pastor! Pastor!"

I walked over and asked him what he had said.

"I called you pastor," he replied. "You're a pastor."

A friend of my wife from another state asked during a phone call, "Is your husband still pastoring a church? I thought he was a pastor."

During a marriage conference, a couple cautiously approached us and asked, "Can we sit at your table? We were hesitant to sit here because we thought you were a pastor."

The final incident occurred on a Sunday morning while we were visiting a church. As the service was ending, I briefly wondered to myself, *When was the last time someone called me pastor?*

One minute later, my wife went to the restroom while I was waiting near the exit. An elderly grandmother walked by with a little girl who was about four years old. The little girl looked at me with a big smile, waved, and said:

"Good-bye, pastor."

None of these things were experiences I was seeking. Yet had it not been for the extended period of fasting, I doubt any of them would have occurred. And I certainly would not have fasted had I arrived at school with all the resources I needed. God orchestrated these circumstances for His purposes.

In my book *Step Into the Supernatural*, I describe many of the miracles and supernatural encounters that occurred during the extended fast, as well as those that followed because of it.

As I look back on that season, I realize that the fast itself was never the point. Hunger was simply the doorway through which God taught me dependence. The circumstances that forced me into fasting—having no money, no food, and no clear path forward—became the very tools God used to draw me closer to Him. In that place of weakness, I began to discover something that cannot be learned from books alone: when a person truly seeks God with humility and sincerity, the Lord is not distant. He is near. He speaks, He guides, and at times He moves in ways that remind us that the spiritual world described in Scripture is not merely historical—it is real.

But the supernatural moments were never meant to become the focus of my faith. They were reminders that God responds when His people humble themselves before Him. The true lesson of that extended fast was not the experiences themselves, but the transformation that occurs when a life is fully surrendered to God. Fasting stripped away my illusions of self-sufficiency and replaced them with a deeper awareness of God's provision and presence. And it is that lesson—far more than any single encounter—that leads us into the deeper purpose of fasting, which we will now reflect upon in the conclusion.

CONCLUSION

Fasting is one of the most misunderstood spiritual disciplines in the modern church. Some treat it as outdated, as if it belonged to a different era of faith. Others treat it like a spiritual lever—something that can be pulled to force results. And still others avoid it altogether because they associate it with extremism, imbalance, or confusion. But when we return to Scripture, we discover something simple and powerful: biblical fasting was never meant to be a spectacle. It was meant to be a surrender.

The Bible shows us repeatedly that fasting is not a fringe practice reserved for a few unusually devoted believers. It appears at some of the most decisive moments in biblical history. Moses fasted before receiving the covenant. Esther fasted before stepping into the king's presence. Nineveh fasted in repentance and mercy was extended. The early church fasted as they ministered to the Lord—and the Holy Spirit spoke with direction and clarity. Even Jesus Himself, though without sin, fasted in the wilderness as He prepared to begin His public ministry. In all of these examples, fasting was not performed to impress men. It was embraced to seek God.

As we have seen throughout this book, fasting is not primarily about food. It is about rulership. The question fasting forces every believer to confront is not merely, "How long can I go without eating?" but rather, "What governs my life?" When we fast, we refuse to allow appetite, whether for food, comfort, distraction, or pleasure—to sit on the throne of the heart. We intentionally quiet the demands of the flesh so that the voice of the Spirit becomes clearer. In that sense, fasting becomes a form of spiritual training. It disciplines the body, exposes the soul, and strengthens the spirit. It does not make us righteous. It makes us honest. It reveals what is truly driving us—and then gives us an opportunity to submit those hidden drivers to God.

That is why fasting, when practiced biblically, produces humility. It is hard to remain prideful when you are reminded of your weakness. It is hard to rely on yourself when your body is hungry and your emotions are exposed. Fasting returns the believer to dependence. It teaches us again what we often forget: we are sustained by God, not by bread alone. The fast becomes a living sermon—preached not from a pulpit, but within the heart—declaring that God is enough.

Yet fasting must also be approached with wisdom. Scripture never encourages recklessness, and discipline was never meant to produce spiritual pride or emotional instability. That is why discernment matters. Not every impression is revelation. Not every intensity is anointing. Not every unusual experience is from God. When fasting increases sensitivity, it must also deepen sobriety. The believer must remain anchored in Scripture, guided by humility, and protected by accountability. True fasting does not lead a person into confusion, arrogance, or obsession with experiences. It leads into greater obedience, deeper love, and a steadier walk with God.

And if there is one message I want you to carry away from this book, it is this: fasting is not a tool to control God. It is a discipline that reorders you. God does not need to be pressured. He needs to be honored. Fasting does not twist His arm—it bends our knee. It does not force His will—it aligns ours. And in that alignment, we begin to see what Scripture has always promised: burdens can be lifted, yokes can be broken, and spiritual clarity can return to a life that once felt clouded by compromise, fear, and distraction.

If you choose to fast, do it prayerfully. Do it responsibly. Do it quietly. And do it with a heart that longs for God more than outcomes. Seek Him first—not merely for what He can do, but for who He is. The greatest reward of fasting is not a story you can tell later. It is a deeper intimacy you carry forward into everyday life.

And when that intimacy becomes your foundation, something else begins to happen. Faith grows. Courage grows. Obedience becomes stronger. And you begin to realize that the Lord is not only calling you to deny the flesh—He is calling you to step out in trust. Fasting strengthens your ability to say no, but faith strengthens your ability to say yes. And in many believers, fasting becomes the quiet preparation for something greater: a life that learns how to move when God speaks, to obey when fear protests, and to walk beyond the natural into the realm where God's power is revealed. That is where the journey continues. Because for many, the discipline of fasting is not the finish line, it is the doorway. And the next step is learning how to **step into the supernatural** by faith.

APPENDIX A

A Comprehensive Biblical Index on Fasting

This appendix provides a structured list of major biblical references concerning fasting for study and research.

Pentateuch

Exodus 34:28
Leviticus 16:29–31
Leviticus 23:27–32
Numbers 29:7
Deuteronomy 9:9
Deuteronomy 9:18
Deuteronomy 9:25

Historical Books

Judges 20:26
1 Samuel 7:6
1 Samuel 31:13
2 Samuel 1:12
2 Samuel 12:16–23
1 Kings 21:27–29
1 Chronicles 10:12
2 Chronicles 20:3

Ezra–Nehemiah

Ezra 8:21–23
Nehemiah 1:4
Nehemiah 9:1

Esther

Esther 4:3
Esther 4:16
Esther 9:31

Psalms

Psalm 35:13
Psalm 69:10
Psalm 109:24

Prophets

Isaiah 58:1–14
Jeremiah 14:12
Jeremiah 36:6
Joel 1:14
Joel 2:12–15
Jonah 3:5–10
Daniel 6:18
Daniel 9:3
Daniel 10:2–3

Zechariah 7:5
Zechariah 8:19

Gospels

Matthew 4:1–2
Matthew 6:16–18
Matthew 9:14–15
Matthew 17:21 (textual variant in some manuscripts)
Mark 2:18–20
Mark 9:29 (textual variant in some manuscripts)
Luke 2:37
Luke 4:1–2
Luke 5:33–35

Acts

Acts 9:9
Acts 10:30
Acts 13:2–3
Acts 14:23
Acts 27:9

Epistles

2 Corinthians 6:5
2 Corinthians 11:27

APPENDIX B

A Practical 30-Day Preparation Plan for a Biblical Fast

This appendix is a preparation guide designed to prepare the believer spiritually, mentally, and physically.

Week 1: Spiritual Inventory

Goal: Examine the heart before beginning.

- Daily prayer of repentance (Psalm 51).
- Identify unresolved bitterness or unforgiveness.
- Ask: What appetite governs me most?
- Journal daily reflections.
- Confess known sin (1 John 1:9).

Week 2: Scriptural Grounding

Goal: Anchor fasting in Scripture.

Daily reading plan:

- Day 1: Isaiah 58
- Day 2: Matthew 6:1–18
- Day 3: Joel 2:12–15

- Day 4: Psalm 35
- Day 5: Daniel 9
- Day 6: Acts 13
- Day 7: Review and journal

Focus: Understand the purpose before the practice.

Week 3: Health and Practical Preparation

Goal: Prepare responsibly.

- Consult a physician if needed.
- Reduce caffeine and sugar gradually.
- Increase water intake.
- Eat lighter meals.
- Establish prayer times.
- Inform accountability partner.

Week 4: Focus and Alignment

Goal: Clarify purpose.

Write down:

- Specific prayer focus.
- Areas needing breakthrough.
- Commitments for humility.

- Plan for breaking the fast gradually.
- Accountability structure.

Prepare spiritually and physically.

Breaking the Fast Properly

- Reintroduce food slowly.
- Avoid overeating.
- Continue prayer rhythm.
- Maintain humility.
- Reflect on lessons learned.
- Record spiritual insights.

Fasting is not an event — it is formation.

APPENDIX C

A 21-Day Guided Fast Companion

A Structured Journey of Preparation, Alignment, and Renewal

Fasting has long been one of the most powerful spiritual disciplines practiced by believers throughout Scripture. From Moses on Mount Sinai, to Esther calling a nation to prayer, to Jesus preparing for ministry in the wilderness, fasting has consistently accompanied moments of deep spiritual preparation and breakthrough.

Yet many believers approach fasting with uncertainty. Questions often arise: *How should I begin? What should I focus on during the fast? How do I remain spiritually engaged throughout the process?*

This **21-Day Guided Fast Companion** is designed to help answer those questions.

It is important to understand that this guide is **not a mandate to fast for twenty-one consecutive days**. Rather, it provides a structured framework to help you prepare your heart, deepen your reflection, and approach fasting with biblical wisdom and humility. Some readers may choose to fast for a shorter period; others may use this guide as preparation before beginning a longer fast.

The purpose of this companion is to help you move beyond simply abstaining from food and into a deeper spiritual encounter with God.

Fasting is not merely about what we give up, it is about what we gain. When physical appetite is quieted, spiritual sensitivity often increases. Prayer becomes more focused. Scripture becomes more alive. The heart becomes more attentive to the voice of God.

Each day of this guide is designed to lead you through a simple but intentional rhythm of reflection and devotion.

Each day includes:

• **A Scripture Focus** to anchor your meditation in God's Word
• **A Devotional Meditation** to guide your spiritual reflection
• **A Prayer Emphasis** to direct your conversation with God
• **A Journal Prompt** to help you record what the Lord is revealing to you

As you move through these days, take your time. Do not rush the process. Fasting is not a race to complete a schedule but an opportunity to cultivate spiritual awareness and dependence on God.

Move slowly. Reflect prayerfully. Write honestly.

Allow the Holy Spirit to use this season to reveal areas of growth, deepen your relationship with God, and strengthen your spiritual life.

May this journey of fasting lead you into greater humility, clarity, and spiritual renewal.

DAY 1 –

The Purpose of the Fast

Scripture: Isaiah 58:6

Meditation:
Biblical fasting is not self-denial for its own sake. It is self-denial for divine alignment. Before you begin, ask yourself: Why am I fasting? Is it for spiritual clarity? Repentance? Direction? Deliverance? The fast must have purpose, or it becomes ritual. God is not impressed by hunger; He responds to humility.

Prayer Focus:
Ask God to purify your motives.

Journal Prompt:
What is my true reason for pursuing a fast in this season?

____

____

____

____

____

____

DAY 2 –

Humility Before God

Scripture: Joel 2:12

Meditation:
Fasting is an act of returning. It is not merely abstaining from food; it is turning the heart back toward God. True fasting rends the heart, not garments. Examine whether there are areas of hidden pride or self-reliance.

Prayer Focus:
Confess pride and ask for humility.

Journal Prompt:
Where have I relied more on myself than on God?

DAY 3 –

Repentance and Cleansing

Scripture: Psalm 51:10

Meditation:
Before the fast begins, cleanse the heart. Unconfessed sin dulls spiritual sensitivity. Repentance restores clarity. David understood that renewal begins within.

Prayer Focus:
Ask God to search and cleanse your heart.

Journal Prompt:
What must I surrender before entering this fast?

____

____

____

____

____

____

DAY 4 –

Dependence on God

Scripture: Matthew 4:4

Meditation:
Man does not live by bread alone. This truth becomes tangible in fasting. Hunger reminds us that physical sustenance is temporary; spiritual sustenance is eternal.

Prayer Focus:
Pray for increased dependence on God's Word.

Journal Prompt:
How does physical hunger mirror spiritual need in my life?

____

____

____

____

____

____

DAY 5 –

Spiritual Awareness

Scripture: 1 Samuel 7:6

Meditation:
Fasting sharpens awareness. Samuel called Israel to fasting and confession before deliverance came. Fasting prepares the heart for God's intervention.

Prayer Focus:
Ask for heightened spiritual sensitivity.

Journal Prompt:
What distractions must be silenced in my life?

____

____

____

____

____

____

DAY 6 –

Aligning with God's Will

Scripture: Acts 13:2–3

Meditation:
The early church fasted while ministering to the Lord—and the Holy Spirit spoke. Fasting creates space for direction.

Prayer Focus:
Seek clarity about current decisions.

Journal Prompt:
What decision in my life requires divine clarity?

____

____

____

____

____

____

DAY 7 –

Breaking Strongholds

Scripture: Isaiah 58:6

Meditation:
The fast loosens bonds. Whether addiction, fear, bitterness, or spiritual stagnation, fasting confronts hidden chains.

Prayer Focus:
Pray for specific areas of deliverance.

Journal Prompt:
What yoke do I need broken?

DAY 8 –

Guarding Against Legalism

Scripture: Matthew 6:16–18

Meditation:
Jesus warned His disciples not to fast for appearance or recognition. In His day, some religious leaders intentionally displayed their fasting through gloomy expressions and public announcements. Their reward was the admiration of others, but they missed the deeper purpose of fasting.

Fasting is never meant to become a spiritual performance. It is not a badge of honor, a tool for impressing others, or a measure of spiritual superiority. True fasting is an act of humility before God.

When fasting becomes legalistic, it loses its power. The heart of fasting is sincere. It is a private act of devotion between you and the Lord.

Jesus taught that fasting should be done quietly, with the focus on God rather than human approval. Your Father sees what is done secretly and responds to the sincere heart.

Prayer Focus:
Ask God to purify your motives so your fasting remains sincere and focused on Him.

Journal Prompt:

Am I fasting to draw closer to God, or am I concerned with how others perceive my spirituality?

DAY 9 –

Submission Before Resistance

Scripture: James 4:7

Meditation:
Scripture teaches a powerful order: *"Submit yourselves therefore to God. Resist the devil, and he will flee from you."*

Many believers attempt to resist spiritual attacks without first surrendering fully to God. But spiritual authority flows from submission. When the heart is surrendered, the believer stands on solid ground against the enemy.

Fasting is an act of submission. It reminds the body that it is not in control and that our lives belong to God. As we humble ourselves through fasting, our spiritual sensitivity increases.

Submission to God strengthens resistance against temptation and spiritual opposition.

Prayer Focus:
Pray for a deeper spirit of surrender and obedience to God's will.

Journal Prompt:
In what areas of my life do I need to surrender more fully to God?

____

____

DAY 10 –

Endurance in Weakness

Scripture: Isaiah 40:31

Meditation:
Fasting often exposes physical weakness. Hunger, fatigue, and emotional fluctuations can surface during extended periods without food.

Yet Scripture reminds us that those who wait upon the Lord renew their strength. Waiting is not passive—it is a posture of trust.

Through fasting, we learn endurance. Instead of relying on physical strength alone, we begin to depend on the sustaining power of God.

The Lord strengthens those who patiently wait on Him.

Prayer Focus:
Pray for endurance and renewed strength during your fast.

Journal Prompt:
What weaknesses have I discovered during this fast, and how can they draw me closer to God?

____

____

____

DAY 11 –

Obedience Over Emotion

Scripture: 1 Samuel 15:22

Meditation:
The prophet Samuel told King Saul that obedience is better than sacrifice. Saul attempted to justify disobedience through religious activity, but God looks beyond outward actions.

Fasting alone does not replace obedience. It is possible to fast yet ignore the voice of God.

True spiritual discipline aligns our actions with God's commands. When fasting is combined with obedience, it becomes a powerful instrument for spiritual growth.

Prayer Focus:
Ask God to help you obey His voice even when it is difficult.

Journal Prompt:
Is there an area where God has asked for obedience that I have been delaying?

____

____

____

____

DAY 12 –

Listening More Than Speaking

Scripture: Ecclesiastes 5:2

Meditation:
Fasting slows us down. Without the normal routines of eating
and social activity, we often become more aware of God's
presence.

Scripture reminds us to be careful with our words before
God. Prayer is not only about speaking; it is also about
listening.

During the fast, create moments of quiet reflection.
Allow the Holy Spirit to speak to your heart through
Scripture and prayer.

Sometimes God speaks most clearly in the silence.

Prayer Focus:
Ask God to open your ears to His voice.

Journal Prompt:
What might God be trying to show me during this time of
fasting?

____

____

____

____

DAY 13 –

Fasting and Compassion

Scripture: Isaiah 58:7

Meditation:
Isaiah teaches that true fasting extends beyond personal devotion. It involves caring for others, feeding the hungry, and helping those in need.

When our hearts align with God, compassion grows naturally. Fasting reminds us of human vulnerability and deepens our empathy toward others.

True fasting transforms not only our relationship with God but also our relationship with people.

Prayer Focus:
Pray for opportunities to demonstrate generosity and compassion.

Journal Prompt:
How can my fasting lead me to serve someone in need?

____

____

____

____

DAY 14 –

Self-Control as Spiritual Fruit

Scripture: Galatians 5:22–23

Meditation:
Self-control is one of the fruits of the Spirit. Fasting strengthens this fruit by training the body to submit to the spirit.

When we deny physical cravings, we learn discipline that extends into other areas of life. The same spiritual strength developed during fasting helps us resist temptation and pursue holiness.

Fasting teaches that our desires do not control us—God does.

Prayer Focus:
Ask the Holy Spirit to cultivate self-control in every area of life.

Journal Prompt:
What areas of my life need greater discipline and spiritual control?

____

____

____

____

DAY 15 –

Corporate Unity

Scripture: Nehemiah 9:1

Meditation:
Throughout Scripture, fasting was often practiced by entire communities. When God's people humbled themselves together, unity was strengthened.

Corporate fasting aligns hearts toward a shared purpose. It reminds believers that spiritual growth is not only personal but communal.

Fasting can strengthen the unity of families, churches, and ministries.

Prayer Focus:
Pray for unity within your church, family, and community.

Journal Prompt:
How can my spiritual discipline contribute to unity among believers?

____

____

____

____

DAY 16 –

Breaking Pride

Scripture: Psalm 35:13

Meditation:
David spoke of humbling his soul through fasting. Pride is one of the greatest obstacles to spiritual growth.

Fasting weakens pride because it reminds us of our dependence on God. We cannot sustain ourselves apart from Him.

Humility opens the door for God's grace and guidance.

Prayer Focus:
Ask God to reveal and remove any pride in your heart.

Journal Prompt:
Where might pride be limiting my spiritual growth?

____

____

____

____

____

DAY 17 –

Strength in Temptation

Scripture: Hebrews 4:15–16

Meditation:
Jesus understands human weakness. He faced temptation yet remained without sin.

During fasting, moments of temptation may arise—not only for food but for impatience, irritation, or discouragement.

Christ invites us to approach the throne of grace for help. His strength sustains us when we feel weak.

Prayer Focus:
Ask God for strength to overcome temptation.

Journal Prompt:
What temptations have surfaced during this fast, and how can I overcome them?

____

____

____

____

____

DAY 18 –

Patience and Timing

Scripture: Ecclesiastes 3:1

Meditation:
Fasting does not force God's hand. Instead, it aligns our hearts with His timing.

Scripture reminds us that everything happens in its season. Answers may not come immediately, but God works according to His perfect schedule.

Patience develops when we trust God's timing more than our own expectations.

Prayer Focus:
Pray for patience while waiting on God's answers.

Journal Prompt:
Where do I need to trust God's timing rather than my own?

____

____

____

____

____

DAY 19 –

Renewed Mind

Scripture: Romans 12:2

Meditation:
Fasting often clears mental distractions and sharpens spiritual focus. As we draw near to God, our thoughts begin to change.

Transformation begins in the mind. When our thinking aligns with Scripture, our behavior follows.

Fasting creates space for God to reshape our perspective and priorities.

Prayer Focus:
Ask God to renew your thoughts and attitudes.

Journal Prompt:
What thought patterns need transformation in my life?

____

____

____

____

____

DAY 20 –

Gratitude in All Things

Scripture: 1 Thessalonians 5:18

Meditation:
Even during physical hunger, fasting can cultivate gratitude. The absence of normal comforts reminds us how much we often take for granted.

Gratitude stabilizes the heart. It shifts our focus from what we lack to what God has already provided.

Thankfulness strengthens faith and deepens trust in God's goodness.

Prayer Focus:
Thank God for His provision, grace, and faithfulness.

Journal Prompt:
What blessings have I recognized more clearly during this fast?

____

____

____

____

DAY 21 –

Consecration and Commitment

Scripture: Romans 12:1

Meditation:
The conclusion of a fast is not the end of spiritual growth, it is a new beginning.

Paul calls believers to present their bodies as living sacrifices to God. This act of consecration represents a life fully dedicated to Him.

Fasting prepares the heart for deeper commitment. As this 21-day journey ends, carry forward the lessons learned during this time of devotion.

Let this season mark a renewed commitment to live faithfully and obediently before God.

Prayer Focus:
Dedicate your life, body, and decisions fully to God.

Journal Prompt:
What commitments will I carry forward from this fast?

____

____

____

____

BIBLIOGRAPHY

This guide is grounded primarily in Scripture. However, the following works have provided theological depth and historical perspective on spiritual discipline and fasting:

Augustine. *Confessions.*
Calvin, John. *Institutes of the Christian Religion.*
Foster, Richard. *Celebration of Discipline.*
Henry, Matthew. *Commentary on the Whole Bible.*
The Didache (Early Christian Teaching).
Spurgeon, Charles. Sermons on Fasting and Prayer.
Wesley, John. "Sermon on Fasting."
Willard, Dallas. *The Spirit of the Disciplines.*

About the Author

Anthony V. Johnson, often called a "Renaissance Man," was born at Fort Benning Army Base, home to prestigious military schools and elite units. Influenced by his father, a Lieutenant Colonel and decorated Vietnam veteran laid to rest at Arlington National Cemetery, Anthony developed a lifelong appreciation for discipline, service, and excellence.

His passion for music began at age seven in Paris, France, and by 14, he was performing in jazz nightclubs. At 17, he joined the Army, earning the nickname "the Singing Corporal" for his cadence calling, later promoted to Sergeant, and served as an Infantry Squad Leader and member of the U.S. Army Mounted Color Guard & Drill Team. He graduated from the rigorous Combat Leader's School at Camp Red Devil and earned the esteemed Expert Infantryman's Badge (EIB).

Anthony's professional journey spans music, law, health physics, and leadership coaching. He performed across Europe and the U.S. in theater musicals, big bands, and various recording acts. As founder of **Quiet Authority™**, he coaches professionals in persuasive communication under pressure. He has also served as a Trial Lawyer and Senior Health Physics Technician at U.S. nuclear facilities, overseeing radiation safety, emergency response, and regulatory compliance.

Anthony holds an A.S. in Business Administration, a B.A. in English, and a Doctor of Jurisprudence. He continues his musical ministry in worship teams across American, Brazilian, and Spanish churches and organized **"A Gathering of the Nations"**, uniting global ministries in multilingual worship. His work in the Spiritual Rights Movement earned him the **Global Leadership Award** from "I Change Nations."

Passionate about aviation, scuba diving, martial arts, travel, and foreign missions, Anthony brings a diverse and adventurous perspective to every pursuit. He can be reached

at: **contact@anthonyvjohnson.com**.
https://anthonyvjohnson.com

Also, by the Author

Fasting Unleashed!
How Prayer and Fasting Destroy Strongholds and Release Breakthrough (2nd Edition) *Available Now*

Fasting Unleashed is your ultimate guide to the transformative practice of biblical fasting. Learn how to unlock divine power and experience spiritual breakthroughs.

- Understand the purpose of fasting and its spiritual impact
- Learn Scripture-based practical fasting steps
- Experience breakthroughs in addiction, fear, anxiety, depression, and generational strongholds
- Unlock favor, healing, and victory over demonic forces

Whether seeking clarity, healing, or renewed purpose, this book equips you to embark on a fasting journey aligned with God's will.

Eternal Security or Eternal Danger: A Biblical Examination of "Once Saved, Always Saved" *Available Now*

Can a single moment of faith guarantee eternal salvation, no matter how we live afterward? Or does the Bible call us to a life of ongoing commitment and obedience?

In this book, you will:

- Discern truth from misconceptions about salvation
- Understand biblical warnings about falling away
- Embrace a balanced, persevering faith

Whether you are a lifelong believer, a curious skeptic, or grappling with your faith, this book offers clarity, conviction, and a challenge to rethink what it truly means to be saved.

Coming Soon!

PSYOPS: The Spiritual Battle for Your Mind and Your Soul! Countdown to Eternity (3rd Edition)

From the moment you were formed in your mother's womb, you entered into spiritual warfare with demonic forces seeking to steal, kill, and destroy your destiny.

Satan engages in PSYOPS (psychological operations) to bring rebellion, confusion, lawlessness, addictions, and separation from God.

- **Part I:** Explore the devil's strategies, tactics, and his first PSYOPS operation.
- **Part II:** Learn heavenly weapons to combat evil, bring healing, deliverance, and fulfill destiny.

Includes review questions, a prayer for deliverance, a checklist for victory, and powerful declarations to guide you on your path to victory.

Step Into the Supernatural:
Taking the First Step of Faith to Unleash Miraculous Breakthroughs

Step into a realm where faith is not theoretical—but lived, demonstrated, and proven. Inspired by the account of the four lepers in 2 Kings 7 and Peter stepping out of the boat onto the water, this book reveals how one act of obedience can activate the supernatural power of God.

Too many believers desire the supernatural… but remain paralyzed by fear, doubt, and hesitation. This book challenges you to move beyond observation and into participation.

• Discover how one step of faith can shift impossible situations
• Break free from fear, hesitation, and spiritual stagnation
• Recognize how God uses ordinary people to produce extraordinary results
• Learn how obedience positions you for sudden and unexpected breakthrough

Whether you are facing a crisis, seeking direction, or longing for a deeper walk with God, this book will show you that your breakthrough may be just one step away.

Premeditated Sin:
Strengthening the Hands of the Enemy

What happens when sin is no longer accidental—but intentional?

In a world where compromise is normalized and conviction is often silenced, this book confronts one of the most dangerous conditions in the life of a believer: premeditated sin.

Drawing from Scripture and real-life insight, this book exposes how deliberate disobedience not only distances us from God, but strengthens the influence of the enemy in our lives.

• Understand the difference between weakness and willful rebellion
• Expose the patterns that lead to spiritual compromise
• Learn how repeated sin dulls conviction and opens doors to deception
• Discover the path back to repentance, restoration, and spiritual authority

Written with the clarity of a courtroom argument and the urgency of a spiritual warning, this book challenges readers to examine their lives honestly and return to a place of true surrender.

Because what is tolerated in private will eventually manifest in public.